Ethical Challenges in Librarianship

ETHICAL CHALLENGES in Librarianship

by Robert Hauptman

Phoenix • New York
ORYX PRESS
1988

The rare Arabian Oryx is believed to have inspired the myth of the unicorn. This desert antelope became virtually extinct in the early 1960s. At that time several groups of international conservationists arranged to have 9 animals sent to the Phoenix Zoo to be the nucleus of a captive breeding herd. Today the Oryx population is nearly 800, and over 400 have been returned to reserves in the Middle East.

Copyright © 1988 by
The Oryx Press
2214 North Central at Encanto
Phoenix, AZ 85004-1483

Published simultaneously in Canada

Printed and Bound in the United States of America

♾ The paper used in this publication meets the minimum requirements of American National Standard for Information Science—Permanence of Paper for Printed Library Materials, ANSI Z39.48, 1984.

Library of Congress Cataloging-in-Publication Data

Hauptman, Robert, 1941–
    Ethical challenges in librarianship / by Robert Hauptman.
      p.   cm.
    Bibliography: p.
    Includes index.
    ISBN 0-89774-271-0
    1. Librarians—Professional ethics. 2. Library science—Moral and ethical aspects. I. Title.
Z682.35.P75H38 1988
174'.9092—dc19   88-1628

"In an increasingly technological and information-intensive society those who manipulate the tools and thereby manipulate the information must be held morally accountable for the power they possess."
Eileen M. Trauth

"The answer to a question, after relentless pursuit, may be obtainable at an unethical price and for most of us it is not worth it."

Patrick M. O'Brien

Contents

Foreword

The subject of ethics is generally considered the material of philosophers and politicians. Their separate discourses are characterized by an inability to make themselves clear. They treat the otherwise common human problem of discovering what is good and bad as a theory so complex as to lack all meaning for the average person, for the average librarian.

Despite the less than winning condition of ethical criticism today, Robert Hauptman gives the readers of his work an extraordinary new approach—an approach that gets to the practical meaning and consequences of ethics in daily library routines. He even dares to define ethics and ethical behavior. His confrontation with tradition and the patriarchy of the library establishment will not please everyone. This seems particularly true because he asks that ethics become a part of library service, not simply a minor point of discussion in a library school course.

When it comes to ethics in libraries, it's hardly a matter of cooking information to serve it up again as disinformation. That's only the stuff of congressional hearings and the after-hours talk of KGB and MI5 agents. No, library ethics are more subtle. They can affect almost every person who walks in and out of a library. Like the ghost of Hamlet's father, they are there and not there, and one can never be sure how to identify ethical shadows. Well, at least until now. Thanks to this imaginative, often brilliant, series of comments by a library ethics "ghostbuster," the reader is able to identify ethical problems.

Ethics is a matter of the good guys and the bad guys. Mr. Hauptman vividly and successfully establishes what this means for librarians. Essentially the librarian must understand the language and motives of the good guys—or exit. Who is to argue? How many people count themselves as evil, out of touch with humanity? The Waste Land blooms, but not in *this* library.

Most of the librarians I know act, or at least try to act, in an ethical fashion. So why bother reading this book? There are several reasons, including Mr. Hauptman's skills as a writer. It is a joy to be caught up in his flights of prose, although most have a hard landing.

Beyond that is the odd idea that all is not well in this, or many other, libraries. The professional experts move 'round the stacks in mistrust. Their findings and articles stir discontent, and no one is more restless than the author of this collection.

Relentlessly, although always with logical caution and even a dash of humor, the author moves from the reference desk to the catalog section to each and every part of the library. His search for ethical problems is rewarded in a sometimes shocking fashion, e.g., read chapter 7, "Censorship."

The atmosphere is not entirely somber. The simple and practical vivacity of suggested solutions, particularly when tied to everyday occurrences in the numerous case studies, destroys the distant theoretical apparatus that sometimes bogs down such discussions. Mr. Hauptman speaks to the reader directly. As he points out in several places, he is not tied to the tyrannical rules of the crowd, or the straightjacket of custom. By nature, training, and experience, Mr. Hauptman is an intellectual. He rightfully expects librarians to share his enthusiasm.

Given that everyone wants to be counted as a good guy, where is the problem? First and foremost, it is a matter of recognition. In his opening chapter Mr. Hauptman carefully points out the need to identify ethical situations—a need too often overlooked.

Nine chapters later, there is a comprehensive set of conclusions and recommendations. Not everyone is going to agree with either the logic or the evidence, but after the succession of practical chapters and case histories, no one is able to ignore the focal point of the argument. The reader is forced to think, if only to argue another type of reform.

The perspectives offered in this well-guided tour are immediate and practical. If librarians find given actions worth doing, they should be for the good. One need not obey a distant voice from above to appreciate the necessity, for example, of offering a legitimate full response to an equally legitimate question or need for material.

We are all in favor of ethical consciousness, no matter how it is obtained. Here it is a matter, as Mr. Hauptman points out, of adequately defining and understanding the good, the right, and the bad. The secret is to be able to associate daily library service with ethics, to make the two virtually synonymous. The author has nobly formulated the problems, suggested answers, and, in the end, offered hope. His ethical view of the world and the library will play a large and useful role in making libraries better places for us all.

Bill Katz
State University of New York at Albany

Preface

This is a book that deals with specific ethical issues. It therefore would be inappropriate for me to assume an entirely neutral stance. Thus, despite the frequent attempt to present issues in conflicting perspectives, the general tenor of this volume, within the traditional boundaries of librarianship, is one of iconoclastic advocacy. At times, my stance is diametrically opposed to general professional positions and American Library Association (ALA) sanctioned principles. Such dissent is operative in all professions, and it must be assumed that this is a healthy attitude, one that ultimately leads to knowledge, wisdom, and improved service.

The case studies that conclude the chapters are entirely fictitious, although some of them are based on actual occurrences.

I take this opportunity to thank Bill Katz for his guidance, John Swan for his interaction, Paul Wiener for his inspiration, and my students for their stimulating, witty, and creative contributions.

Ethical Challenges in Librarianship

Chapter 1
Ethics and Librarianship

Because of the life and death situations that a doctor frequently encounters and the confidence and trust placed in one's lawyer, ethical considerations have always played a seminal role within these traditional professions. Far too often, members of many groups, professional or not, have failed to comport themselves in an ethical manner. In short, businesspeople, auto mechanics, scientists, and even doctors and lawyers have allowed economic, social, or other ends to justify unacceptable or unethical means.

Until recently, librarians and information professionals gave very little thought to ethical problems. The literature prior to the mid-seventies is replete with discussions of manners, etiquette, and decorum, but there is little available on specific ethical issues. Recently, ethical considerations have come to play an increasingly important role in all areas—from politics and applied scientific research to business and advertising practices—and this has stimulated information specialists to begin to consider their specific domain within an ethical context.

GENERAL ETHICAL PRINCIPLES

Aristotle, Spinoza, Kant, and a host of other philosophers have discoursed at length on a diversity of tenable ethical theories. Although these are usually not discussed in commentaries on applied ethics (in areas like business, journalism, politics, or medicine), the underlying principles, derived from the writings of theorists, are invariably subtly operative. The basic ethical superstructure for this study is an eclectic mixture of various ethical systems, with an emphasis on common sense.

An applied ethics will hardly be viable if it is not at least partially utilitarian and pragmatic. At the same time, a structure devoid of any underlying principles will be so open-ended as to make virtually any action defensible. This is perhaps one of the primary problems with Joseph Fletcher's situation ethics. Kant, in his *Fundamental Principles of the Metaphysics of Morals*, elucidates a sound and generally acceptable group of axioms that can provide basic guidance here. The first of these is what Kant terms a good will. For the purposes of this study, a good will can be construed as the *desire* to act correctly, fairly, or ethically. Second, Kant cites duty (or adherence to the law). Today, except perhaps in government work, especially in the secret service or the military, acting purely out of duty does not carry the positive aura that it did in the eighteenth century. Nevertheless, this axiom can be useful here if duty is thought of as either personal or, more appropriately, professional obligation. Third is the famous categorical imperative—the requirement always to act so that the action can be universalized (without harmful results). Theoretically, this sounds excellent, but of course in real, everyday situations, one may have to choose between two basically "universalizable" actions. Finally, and most cogent, is the dictum to always treat human beings as ends and never merely as means. (passim) In other words, always consider the dignity and human worth of each individual.

These Kantian axioms are generally applicable in both ordinary and professional interchanges between human beings. But professionals have a number of additional specific ethical obligations to their clients. Michael D. Bayles's effective discussion of these provides the basis for the following summary. Obligations are of three types. First come standards, which simply indicate that one should aspire to certain characteristics, e.g., knowledge, honesty, and competence. Standards are not prescriptive. Second are principles of responsibility. These obligations delimit, but still leave room for discretion, e.g., it is the responsibility of an information specialist to provide factually correct material, but the manner in which this is located and the sources used are discretionary. Finally, there are rules of duty. Here one is bound, perhaps even legally, to act in a specific way. (22–23) For example, it is the duty of personnel to maintain the confidentiality of circulation records.

It is when two diametrically opposed obligations conflict with each other that one encounters an ethical dilemma, the resolution of which can be reached only by weighing and evaluating the importance of the conflicting obligations. This is often a painfully difficult procedure.

The reason that these ethical dilemmas arise is that there is no obvious and absolute resolution to problems. Two or more equally valid solutions pull the librarian in antithetical directions. Thus, no truly casuistic set of rules or regulations can provide for every contingency. As Stephen Toulmin admonishes, an absolute adherence to mere principle is ethically counterproductive. Discretion is mandatory. (38) The individual must make a choice, based on careful deliberation of the situation, and then bear responsibility for his or her actions. This is not just existential jargon. This is what life is all about. It is impossible for mature, responsible human beings (especially professionals, because of their extraordinary obligations) to simply allow the responsibility of decision making to devolve upon administrators, superiors, religious organizations, or the ALA and its code of ethics. The Nuremberg Trials and Stanley Milgrim's experiments (carefully delineated in *Obedience to Authority*) have shown unequivocally that that will not suffice—legally, ethically, or humanly.

THE TWO PERSPECTIVES

It will undoubtedly come as a surprise to most readers that in the dynamic and complex area of information ethics, many controversies can be reduced to two diametrically opposed positions. There is the traditional point of view, advocated by D. J. Foskett back in 1962, that the personal beliefs of the librarian must not under any circumstances influence his or her professional duties: "no politics, no religion, no morals," is how Foskett puts it (passim).

The etiology for this is bifurcate. First, the information specialist exists to help patrons locate information, not to advocate particular viewpoints or to make moral judgments. Taken superficially, this seems fair and commendable. Second, until fairly recently, scientists have been interested only in discovery, abjuring responsibility for the detrimental technological applications of their work. The laboratory scientist was viewed as an amoral creature, and because science is the paradigm for all good things in the modern world, so must the information specialist emulate this amoral stance.

But during the last 50 years there has been a subtle shift in attitude among scientists. Ever since Einstein wrote his famous letter to President Roosevelt concerning the use of the atomic bomb, scientists and the scientific community have attempted, with perhaps limited success, to bear responsibility for their work. The point is that there *is* a strict connection between the laboratory and the external inhabited world. Analogously, there is an undeniable connection between provided information and its application or use. The amorality of information provision remains the official professional position, advocated by ALA and many of those who take an interest in this area. John Swan is one of the most articulate defenders of the patron's right to unimpeded access to information: Neither ethical considerations nor any form of censorship should be allowed to obstruct or forestall the free flow of information. (Wiener passim) This, of course, is Foskett's traditional position, readvocated here a quarter of a century later.

Diametrically opposed to this traditional perspective is an icono-clastic advocacy of specific and individual decision making, and the necessity of bearing full responsibility for one's actions. One of its earliest manifestations is my infamous 1976 bomb experiment, in which requests for information on the chemical properties of cordite (requests made with the strong implication that a suburban house was to be blown up) to 13 libraries were generally eagerly fulfilled. The theoretical conclusion of the resulting essay is that this excellent service is ethically reprehensible, that the abjuring of social respon-sibility in favor of the dubious professional commitment of dispens-ing information is ethically unacceptable (Hauptman, "Profession-alism" passim).

Subsequently, occasional lone voices have been raised in partial agreement with this stance. One of the most unusual is Lydia F. Knight's. In a lengthy letter published in *Library Journal*, she disagrees with some case analyses and then goes on to discuss censorship and intellectual freedom. Her point of departure is the Judeo-Christian ethic (she has obviously failed to read Foskett). She asks fairly, "Must I live a dichotomous life, adhering to one set of standards in my professional life and to another in my private life?" (9) The answer is, Yes, of course, she must. This is precisely what "professionalism" demands. (Professional prerequisites and abuses are discussed in chapter 2.) Knight's dichotomy is an excellent example of an ethical dilemma—one that is not easily solvable by application to organizational dictates or a casuistic code.

There is an interesting sidelight to all of this. During the spring of 1987, Robert C. Dowd, a graduate student at the State University of New York at Albany, essentially repeated the bomb experiment, but with one major difference. Instead of asking for information on the chemical properties of cordite, he attempted to discover how to freebase cocaine, an illegal and dangerous activity. Dowd dressed the part of a drug abuser, looked suspicious, acted hesitantly, spoke quietly and concisely, and strongly implied that he planned to try freebasing once he learned how to do so. Dowd's results are consis-tent with the original experiment: Not a single librarian refused to render assistance, although one did respond immediately, "We don't provide instructions on how to do that." She subsequently did at-tempt to help locate the information.

Dowd made three additional discoveries: None of the consulted information specialists held a reference interview, nor did they pro-vide any bibliographic instruction; and a few were only grudgingly helpful. (passim) The implications of this study are either that librar-ians still give little thought to ethical problems, or they adhere so stringently to the ALA code that the nature of the request is indeed entirely irrelevant.

CODES OF ETHICS

In their documentary history of American library codes of ethics, Jonathan A. Lindsey and Ann E. Prentice remark that

> codes of ethics, or even official statements on the part of library associations, have not been burning professional issues during the several centuries of American librarianship. The question appears to have been irrelevant prior to 1900, and some would say that it has been of little relevance since. (19)

As early as 1903, Mary W. Plummer noted a group of ethical concerns in a document that was largely ignored by the profession. By 1929–1930, a suggested code reached the ALA constituency, but it was not until 1938 that a code of ethics was finally adopted by the ALA. (Lindsey, 20, 35, 40, 42) Here at last was an attempt to regulate the ethics of the profession by clearly articulating the tasks and obligations of the librarian in an accessible and ALA-sanctioned document. If it was overly long, concerned with irrelevancies, not particularly useful in a difficult situation, and unenforceable, at least it was indicative of a professional interest in correct action. Its impact, however, was slight. From 1960 until 1973, many suggestions and proposals were made, and in 1975 a new "Statement on Professional Ethics" was adopted by the ALA. (53) This was a concise, well-meaning document that, taken with the *Library Bill of Rights* and the *Freedom to Read Statement* (Lindsey), provided a fair guide for the profession. But like its predecessor, it was of no real help when one was faced with a trying dilemma, and, of course, it remained unenforceable.

The profession now operates under the "Statement on Professional Ethics 1981" (Lindsey), which consists of a concise introduction followed by a six-point code. (63–64) The preliminary comments are praiseworthy, since they affirm a commitment to flexibility, intellectual freedom, access to information, and personal integrity. There can be little argument with all but the fifth point in the actual code. The first insists on the provision of excellent service. Number 2 decries censorship. Number 3 covers confidentiality. Number 4 adjures librarians to treat each other fairly. Number 6 warns against conflict of interest. Number 5, however, perpetuates the myth that personal and professional ethical commitments are incompatible, a view that causes many problems that plague information services.

Despite the divisive nature of the fifth principle as well as the code's failure to insist upon individual responsibility for one's actions, it does protect the patron, the collection, and the librarian's peers. It does *not* attempt to protect the profession at the expense of the client. Thus, all in all, this too is a commendable, if neither extremely useful nor enforceable, document. One would think that it is certainly better than nothing at all, providing as it does educational and paradigmatic guidance. Samuel Rothstein might disagree. In 1968, commenting on the then-operative 1939 code, he insisted that it was meaningless, consisting as it did of "fatuous adjurations" and rhetorical preening. He continued,

> Let's face it, librarians, unlike lawyers, doctors, bankers, and politicos, have precious little opportunity to steal or do other serious disservice to our clients. (156,157)

He believed that codes are not particularly relevant to the problems with which librarians must contend. He therefore suggested that the code be replaced by an ethos, a center out of which librarians could operate effectively.

Even in 1979, when I thus summarized it, Rothstein's position was interesting but untenable (Hauptman, "Ethical" 198). Today, with the extensive development of information services and many new ethical problems, a well-defined code is a necessity. Lisa Newton summarizes the situation incisively:

> The essential function of the code is to encourage criticism, especially self-criticism, among the practitioners supposedly "bound" by it. The ethic of the professional is to be found in the dialectical interaction between the conscience of the individual professional and the collective conclusions of the profession as a whole, and the formulations of the "Professional Code," always provisional and continually being revised, are the medium of that dialectical process. (40)

COMPLIANCE

Doctors are licensed by the state and bound by the Hippocratic oath, as well as by the strictures of the American Medical Association (AMA). If medical practitioners stray too far from the prescribed way of doing things, they can be admonished by the AMA or lose their mandatory licenses, without which doctors cannot legally practice medicine. The same principle holds for clergy, who may be defrocked, and lawyers, who may be disbarred, if they do not act in accordance with professional dictates. This is precisely what happened to the well-known lawyer Roy M. Cohn, whose consistently unethical practices finally led to his disbarment. Disbarment, of course, makes it impossible for a lawyer to continue to practice. Pressure even can be brought to bear upon nonprofessionals like automobile mechanics or plumbers by their respective organizations or by consumer protection groups. Eventually, incompetent or dishonest service persons will lose their jobs or be forced to go out of business. This, of course, does not mean that unethical actions do not occur with great frequency. Watergate, Abscam, Irangate, stock market scandals, and fiction masquerading as journalism, among many other examples, indicate how widespread unethical activity is. But in each case, there is some form of redress available once the truth comes to light. At the highest levels, a president can be forced to resign; some perpetrators may be tried and jailed; others are sued and must relinquish large sums of money of money; still others can lose their jobs.

What forces the librarian to comply with organizational regulations, professional dictates, or the ALA code? What regulates the librarian's ethical compliance? Simply put, nothing does. Naturally, individuals must adhere to the rules of the organization that pays their salaries. Problems of an ethical nature arise only infrequently, and when they do, they are probably worked out through discussion or mediation. It is an unlikely situation in which a blatantly unethical act results in immediate dismissal. Of course, some employees or directors steal books or embezzle funds, but such crimes are not peculiar to librarianship. Various librarians with differing philosophies can and do function autonomously with respect to ethics in the same organization. They may even act in diametrically opposed ways without suffering negative results. This does not usually occur in medicine or in law, where the rules are precise and the practitioners are accountable for adhering to them.

Librarians are not licensed (with the exception of school librarians), and many do not even belong to the ALA or a state library association. Thus, there is no controlling body that can enforce compliance with legal or professional dictates or codes. Whereas the state and the AMA have substantial power over all medical doctors, neither the state nor the ALA has any power over librarians. Even ALA members are not compelled to act in accordance with the code.

Peer pressure cannot be cited as a possible enforcer, since in a given ethical situation (unless it is a clear-cut example of dishonesty, such as embezzlement or vandalism—in which case it becomes a legal matter), one's peers are likely to align themselves into two camps: Some will think that the action is ethically unacceptable, while others will disagree. But even if all of one's peers think that one has acted unethically, only an employer can insist that changes be made. Peers and the ALA are powerless to enforce compliance.

It is certainly ironic that such a large, wealthy, and powerful organization as the ALA has absolutely no power over its members or over librarians generally. This is perhaps one of the greatest impediments to full professional status for librarians, at least in the eyes of lay persons. In librarianship, compliance with professional ethical norms derives not from authority but rather from the individual's conscience—and since librarians are taught to demarcate professional activity from personal beliefs, ethical foundations are grounded in paradox. It is thus hardly surprising that, even today, ethical concerns are of no great import in schools of librarianship or in the workplace.

CONSEQUENCES

One of the greatest problems here is the inability of the profession (despite its code) to reach consensus on what, in a given situation, constitutes unethical behavior. In a certain sense, this can be true in medicine or law as well. Consider the situation in which a lawyer must either defend the confessed perpetrator of a heinous deed or go to jail for refusing (once he or she has already undertaken the case). Some lawyers, despite the legal and presumably ethical directive, have chosen jail. In librarianship, Foskett (passim) and Swan (Wiener, passim) would insist, it is unethical to fail to provide information in virtually all cases, whereas Hauptman and Knight would hold that there are situations in which the very same provision of information constitutes unethical activity. Theoretically, it does not matter which choice is made—to provide information or not—since there are no absolute consequences. A superior may (or may not) chastise the librarian, but no disbarment or defrocking will follow. Only in legally actionable cases will an absolute consequence likely follow, i.e., arrest, trial, and sentencing.

There is a new wrinkle to this, one that has been plaguing other professionals for some time, but which has just begun to have an impact upon information specialists. This is the malpractice suit. Malpractice actions can result from unethical activity, but incompetence is probably a more frequent cause, and it is incompetent information provision that will probably bring the malpractice suit into the world of librarianship. Actual suits would have very different results if brought against public, school, academic, or special librarians or against commercial information brokers. Against the latter, who charge considerable fees for their services, suits have already been won. A public or school librarian (who does not charge for services rendered) would probably win, if a case actually ever did get to court. This is all quite hypothetical, since, although the negligence of doctors harms more than 100,000 people per year ("Reports," 6A) and suits are common, few if any malpractice suits have been brought against librarians.* (See chapter 9 for further comments on malpractice.)

---

*A 1986 amendment to an Illinois law protects librarians from malpractice suits brought because of injury that resulted from provided information (*ILL. ANN. STAT. 85:2–107* and *2–210*).

CASE STUDY

Sam Monteel rushed into the director's office, exclaiming as he slammed the fragile glass door behind him, "That demanding old man, Mr. Lully, whom we help so frequently with stock and bond statistics, is threatening to sue us for malpractice. He has already consulted his lawyer."

Rachel Binton was a competent reference librarian and an excellent administrator. She had been the director of this large public library for five years, and was well aware of Mr. Lully's obstreperous and demanding nature. She had thought, however, that the services that the library rendered had helped to make him fairly wealthy. She asked for the details.

It turned out that, based upon the printed form of an annual report (which the library supplied without charge from a compact disk), financial information gleaned from *Moody's Industrials*, and especially from some interpretive commentary on daily stock prices and information contained in *Value Line*, which Monteel perhaps foolishly had offered, Mr. Lully had lost a considerable sum in the stock market. Curmudgeonly Mr. Lully, during the past three years, had kept careful track of the advice that various librarians had tendered. He now could show that about 40 percent of the information was either false or misleading. As long as he had been successful in his investments, he had not cared. But now he threatened to use this evidence in a suit brought against both the library and the two librarians who had been most culpable.

It was little consolation to the director that suits against municipal entities were difficult to win. In reality, she thought that if things went just right, Mr. Lully very well could win. The publicity would be extremely negative, and it would set a terrible precedent, even if the library won. But what could be done? All of the reference personnel were competent and attempted to help the patrons to the best of their abilities. Apparently, however, that was not good enough, since national statistics gathered in studies indicate that about half of all queries are answered incorrectly. She could promise Mr. Lully to do a better job in the future or ask him to seek his financial advice from professional stockbrokers.

She talked some of these ideas over with Monteel, who seemed beside himself and really had nothing to contribute. Monteel was opening the door to leave when he was almost run down by Mr. Lully, who rushed across the room and began threatening to immediately file a suit against the library for $200,000 unless something was done.

1. How could this entire brouhaha have been avoided?
2. Is financial advice, in a certain sense, similar to medical and legal advice?

3. How can this situation be defused?
4. What will be the result of an actual suit?
5. Do you suppose that the library carries malpractice insurance? How about the individual librarians?

CASE STUDY*

Frank Ludlow was in his fifth year as a reference librarian at a small but prestigious college which maintained a valuable and nationally recognized collection of specialized materials and rare books. Ludlow, an exemplary employee, believed that one should never give up in the attempt to answer a reference question. He was justifiably proud of his ability to ferret out whatever information was requested, even if he had to work on a problem over an extended period of time. Because of his attitude, many professors availed themselves of his services whenever they had especially difficult research tasks to accomplish. He was so highly esteemed that occasionally reference personnel at other nearby academic institutions forwarded unsolvable questions to him. He was, additionally, active in state and national professional organizations. His special area of interest was intellectual freedom.

One hot and humid summer afternoon, when things were slow and quiet, despite the air-conditioned pleasantness that the library offered, a well-dressed and rather aristocratic man approached Ludlow with a series of questions concerning library protection systems. Eventually, they wended their intellectual way to the specific system and devices used to protect the college's invaluable rare books and manuscripts. Ludlow was all aglow: just two years before, he had investigated library security systems as the head of an ad hoc committee whose purpose was to choose and install the best system available. Ludlow, therefore, had most of the bibliographic citations immediately at hand and these he passed along to the patron. He then launched into a detailed description of the dual system that they had purchased and indicated that in the event of failure of one portion, the other would continue to function. The committee had concluded that the various collections (and especially those sacred items stored in the vault) were as safe as the gold in the Federal Reserve Bank in New York City. The patron gobbled up all of this detailed information, taking notes and asking intelligent follow-up questions. After about 40 minutes, he thanked Ludlow, excused himself, and left the building.

On the Monday morning following the Thanksgiving holiday, Salvatore Crichton, special collections librarian, opened the door to

---

*The idea for this case derives from a comment made by Robert C. Dowd.

his beloved sanctuary and gaped with abject horror at the partially bare bookcases that ran from floor to ceiling around the entire large room. He walked up and down along the walls, glancing at what remained of the college's precious rare books and manuscript collection. He was astounded to note that the best and most valuable volumes, the rarest first editions, and even the books with the finest provenances were gone, whereas the less valuable and interesting material remained. He immediately realized that only someone who knew the rare-book market and this particular collection could have done such a scrupulous job. He rushed to the vault and almost fainted when he saw that the door was ajar. The he recalled the security system and wondered why it had not alerted the police. "My God," he exclaimed, "this is an inside job, and I'm the one they will suspect." Word soon travelled across campus, and librarians, professors, and students trooped in to see the damage for themselves.

That afternoon, Ludlow called the library director and asked for an immediate appointment. After the usual courtesies, Ludlow described the patron he had helped the previous summer and recounted the detailed information he had provided concerning the security system. He also pointed out that he had not discussed the actual collections at all. As he spoke, the director became more and more agitated, and by the time the story was completed, he was visibly shaken and extremely angry.

"How could you reveal the intimate details of the system to a complete stranger?" The director asked. "That was privileged information, top secret, and not available to anyone who happens to wander onto our campus."

"But my job is to dispense information," Ludlow said. "No one ever proscribed those details. No one ever specifically forbade the committee members from revealing it. I was simply helping a patron. I was just doing my job."

The director was too upset to continue. He stood up to dismiss Ludlow. "Listen," he said. "You will have to repeat all of this to the police and the insurance investigators. But I still cannot understand how you could be so ingenuous, how you could fail to realize that that information was not for public consumption, how you could avoid making a judicious professional decision to refuse to help someone steal our books."

Ludlow knew how he felt, but he did not want to alienate the director further by citing ALA dicta and his own belief that reference personnel were paid to provide information, not to pry into motives. He had been taught to help patrons and that is what he had done.

1. Ludlow ignored personal responsibility in favor of an absolute dictum. Was he wrong in principle to do so? In fact?
2. Are there limits to intellectual freedom and the commitment to dispense information?
3. Is "doing one's job" an adequate defense, especially for a professional, in the face of social or institutional detriment?

Chapter 2
Professing Professionalism*

Samuel Johnson was wrong: Lexicographers are not harmless drudges; they are masochists. The speaking and writing public distorts and abuses words and their putative meanings so egregiously that they often become virtually useless in traditional contexts. The term "science" comes immediately to mind, as does "profession" and its many lexicographical derivatives. As there were three hard sciences—physics, chemistry, and more recently biology—so too were there three professions—medicine, law, and theology.

Because professionals are generally well-remunerated, respected, and honored, the practitioners of countless occupations have aspired to professional status. Indeed, the professionalization of Western society is a never-ending process, despite many occupations' lack of necessary requirements. Thieves, plumbers, truck drivers, master printers, and computer programmers simply declare themselves professionals, and it is so. It matters little that one or more of the prerequisites for professional status is absent. If lengthy training, an intellectual component (a theoretical body of knowledge), service, a strong and enforceable ethical commitment and code, autonomy, or remuneration, at least in the form of prestige or public recognition, is lacking, so much the better. The new professions are forward-looking; they can do without all of the traditional baggage.

Of course, the popular usage of the term "professional" has nothing to do with the traditional professions. Thus, there are professional taxi drivers, professional prostitutes, and professional stockbrokers, ad infinitum. On the other hand, there are some occupational groups that did conform to the traditional professional model. Today their practitioners are legitimate professionals in the precise meaning of the term: Educators, dentists, and research scientists are excellent examples.

---

*Part of this chapter derives from Fred Hill and Robert Hauptman's "Deride, Abide, or Dissent: On the Ethics of Professional Conduct," unpublished.

To define the professions thus, in terms of attributes, is to subscribe to the functionalist method. Lisa Newton points out that there is another sociological approach to this problem, one in which the cynical assume that professionalism is a myth promulgated solely to reap "social and economic advantages." (33) These critics insist that prerequisites, attributes, attitudes, criteria, and objectives are all instituted to benefit the individual members of the profession and not to aid clients. Codes, for example, are merely a manifestation of the ideology, a public-relations ploy (34), and superfluous, since the professions are "amoral economic pressure groups immune from ethical concerns." (37)

John Kultgen discusses four purported ideological myths (independence, altruism, peer review, wisdom) promulgated by the professions. Through judicious commentary, he demonstrates that these principles upon which the professions base their claims to special rights and privileges do not truly represent reality. (62–64) The cynical attitude that Newton describes derives from a Marxist perspective and the necessity to reduce all classes, groups, and strata to the same level. There can be little doubt that some of the criticism is valid, but such extreme and inflexible conclusions hardly seem tenable. Kultgen's presentation of the same hypercritical attitude results in a more balanced conclusion.

LIBRARIANSHIP

Professionals are either consultants or scholars (Bayles, 9). Consultants, such as doctors, lawyers, and engineers, often serve and subsequently are remunerated by individual clients. Scholars, including teachers and researchers, work for large organizations, do not deal with individual clients, and are remunerated by the organization.

Librarianship is anomalous. It falls, logically enough, into the scholarly category, and some librarians (catalogers, bibliographers, selectors, collection developers) do not usually deal with clients. But others (access service or reference personnel) consistently interact with patrons. And to further complicate matters, a limited number from both groups instruct in regular programs. This is the case, for example, at Evergreen State College (Olympia, WA), where librarians teach various courses on a rotating basis, or at St. Cloud State University (St. Cloud, MN), where librarians teach as part of their usual workload in regular B.A. and M.A. programs. Of course, virtually all librarians are compensated by an organization. They do not work for commissions or fees.

Librarians long ago proclaimed themselves professionals. Whether they are is a moot point, and therefore it is often debated in the literature. Most commentators conclude that professional status is deserved, while only a few iconoclasts continue to fault librarianship for lacking a true and necessary intellectual component and an *enforceable* ethical code. The former may never evolve, simply because general library services do not require an extensive body of theoretical knowledge for their commission. To be a general medical practitioner, one must master biochemistry, anatomy, physiology, histology, pharmacology, and so on. Specialists in surgery, psychiatry, or sports medicine require further training. This is obviously analogously the case for both lawyers and clergy, although perhaps to a lesser degree. It is emphatically not the case in librarianship, and all of the harrumphing and preening by the egotistical will not change matters. A clerk or secretary cannot fill in for an ailing surgeon or trial lawyer—neither legally nor practically. A competent paraprofessional probably can do virtually any job within the library field except for administration or esoteric selection, where substantive knowledge of another discipline is required.

As for the code, it exists, but since adherence is entirely at one's personal discretion, it is unenforceable. This appears to leave librarians precariously balanced on the brink of professional status, although in practice librarians are frequently viewed as professionals and accorded the appropriate privileges and status.

At one time, ethical training was an integral part of the college experience. But, as Frederick H. Borsch notes, this is certainly no longer the case: It is now extremely difficult to impart specific values or even to indicate something about their etiology, since colleges and universities are ostensibly value-neutral. Despite this difficulty on the undergraduate level, however, ethical concerns now *are* an integral part of the training of doctors, lawyers, and clergy, and more recently of engineers, M.B.A.s, psychologists, and even research scientists. This is still not the case in training for library or information service. Educators seem to think that other matters must take precedence during a master's program of limited duration, since ethics, at least superficially, does not appear to be of great moment within librarianship.

This misconception should be put to rest. Ethical behavior is a prerequisite for sustained good relations in any human activity, occupation, or profession, and librarianship is no exception. If cataloging, classification, reference, or computer-searching is not taught within an ethical context, then ethical concerns assuredly will be ignored after graduation, during day-to-day operations. Furthermore, if practitioners are unaware of or take little interest in the ethical obligations of the profession, they will fail to pass these obligations on to paraprofessional or clerical helpers. Thus, the nonprofessional, for example, will continue to innocently divulge the names of patrons who happen to have material checked out or attempt to censor items that are personally offensive.

ANTI-PROFESSIONALISM

Professional ethics may never displace ordinary ethics. The former, at times, can be different from the latter, but this must never give professionals an unfair advantage over either nonpractitioners of their profession or clients. The Kantian axioms and the obligations discussed earlier work both ways. For example, just as the professional is obliged to maintain standards, principles of responsibility, and rules of duty, so, too, in a less stringent manner, must library patrons comport themselves in an acceptable fashion, present accurate information, and pay for certain services. The point is that the professional/client relationship is a mutually ethical endeavor and should never be construed so as to allow professionals to abuse their calling. A dichotomy between professional behavior and what is normally taken to be true or good is ethically unacceptable.

The perspective that allows one to distinguish between the professional and the acceptable can be termed, according to Stanley Fish, anti-professionalism (89), a concept that subsumes professional dissent and whistle blowing. The characteristics that Fish associates with the anti-professional (care, responsibility, freedom, sincerity), of course, should be attributes of the professional, but this, lamentably, is often not the case. It is of no consequence theoretically whether the activity is subtle and legal or blatant and illegal. If it is dichotomous, i.e., if the professional behavior contravenes the normally good or acceptable, it is unethical. Take Bayles's example of professional fee schedules (now illegal), which ostensibly protected the client from less effective work at a lower cost. As Bayles observes, fee schedules eliminate competition, and the client is forced to pay a minimum fee regardless of the service rendered. (33) Other examples of unethical compensation structuring include fee splitting and the prohibition against competitive bidding. (34) These are among the many subtle ways that professionals manipulate matters so that certain behaviors are deemed unprofessional, presumably to protect the client, but in reality to give an unfair (and therefore unethical) advantage to the professional.

As disconcerting as this type of activity is (and it remains pervasive through all of the professions), it is mere tomfoolery compared with examples discussed by Burton J. Bledstein in his incisive study, *The Culture of Professionalism*. Here one discovers that during the 1890s, conservative medical practitioners defended "the containment of the poor in the ghettos" and "refused to cooperate with public boards of health which required the reporting of tuberculosis cases." (93) And even worse,

> gynecologists and psychiatrists diagnosed female hysteria as a pathological problem with a scientific etiology related to an individual's physical history rather than anger the public by suggesting that it

was a cultural problem related to dissatisfied females in the middle-class home. (330)

This type of behavior indicates that professionals can be uncaring, socially irresponsible, untrustworthy, self-promoting, greedy, and dishonest, then defend themselves by working the unacceptable or unethical behavior patterns into their professional codes as ostensibly positive necessities. But it is a given that if there is a conflict between professional demands and ordinary ethics, the latter must prevail.

A SURVEY

To ascertain the extent of ethical concerns in the professions generally, Fred Hill and I surveyed 11 different professional groups, from each of which 50 practitioners were chosen arbitrarily from directories. Of the 550 questionnaires sent out, only 64 were returned. This in itself is a telling comment on the professional's interest in ethical matters. The following list indicates the number of respondents from each group.

- Speech Communication Personnel   0
- Politicians   1
- Medical Practitioners   1
- Military   4
- Information Scientists   5
- Lawyers   6
- Academicians   9
- Clergy   9
- Business Personnel   9
- Engineers   10
- Psychologists   10

Precise details, hypotheses, results, and explanations are included in the complete paper. Here it is sufficient to note that although only six of the 64 respondents indicated that they would contravene their respective codes (18 were familiar with specific examples of such contravention), 21 (almost a third) had dissented professionally in one way or another, sometimes with repercussions including the loss of their jobs. The explanation for this may be that these professionals sincerely believe that their respective codes are positive guides to ethical behavior. Furthermore, since they made the effort to return the questionnaire, one might infer that these are caring, responsible people, and when faced with a negative situation, they felt compelled to react by blowing the whistle or refusing to follow an order.

The results of this survey have a significant impact on the ethical foundations of library service. Consider the bomb experiment cited earlier. According to professional dictates, reference personnel are obliged to provide information without considering its application. As John Swan convincingly argues, without the proper information the patron cannot make his or her own ethical decision (Wiener, 162). Nevertheless, once the librarian realizes or even suspects that the information will be used for anti-social purposes—the destruction of property or lives—then professional dictates must become subservient to ordinary ethics, which require one to honor property and lives. Otherwise the information specialist is blatantly ignoring his or her social responsibility, by citing a professional code, and aiding and abetting socially deleterious, as well as illegal, activity. The professional commitment to dispense information is a praiseworthy objective, as long as it does not conflict with ordinary human values.

CASE STUDY

Carolus Shalum immigrated to the United States when he was 17 years old. Through perseverance and diligence he became fluent in English and, despite financial problems, managed to graduate from high school. For 10 years, he had worked as a clerk and page in a southern state's legislative law library, which served both legislators and the general public. His work was impeccable, and he was well-liked by co-workers and the many senators and representatives who passed through the library. Because of his duties, Shalum quickly became interested in legal matters and spent much of his personal time reading, studying, and assimilating legal materials, so that he soon became extremely knowledgeable about virtually all aspects of American law. He had thought about going to college and then to law school, but he never quite got around to making a commitment. And now, he thought, he was too old to do so. Besides, he liked his work, earned enough money to live, and spent his free time contentedly memorizing precedents and solving mock cases.

In the fall of 1983, there were a number of simultaneous crises with which the legislature had to cope. The regular reference librarians were overwhelmed and for weeks had been working extra hours without additional compensation. On a particularly busy morning the phone rang continually, and on one occasion Shalum happened to answer. It was one of the most powerful senators, whose impact was often felt at the national level. He needed a brief on a local case that had gone on to the United States Supreme Court. He also wanted some interpretive commentary. Shalum said that he would have it all ready by two o'clock. By quickly finishing up most of his appointed tasks, and then working feverishly through his lunch hour, Shalum managed to gather the requested materials, make some photocopies, search out some commentary, and even write and type a short synopsis. He delivered all of this at 2:00 P.M.

About two weeks later, this same senator was passing through the library and happened to spot Sara Conkley, the head of reference. He complimented her on the superb and efficient work that Shalum had done for him. She thanked him, returned to her office, and summoned Shalum.

"I have just had some praise for the work that you did for the senator," she said. "But you know that only the professionally trained librarians are supposed to do that type of research. And even they do not make a habit of summarizing or interpreting. Everyone is aware that you know more than some lawyers, but even competent nonprofessionals are not allowed to render reference service."

Shalum was disheartened. Never before had he been reprimanded. "But if I am capable, why can't I have the opportunity to contribute, especially since we have been so busy?" he asked.

"We have to abide by the rules. The librarians who have master's degrees and in some cases are also lawyers will not put up with competition from a mere high school graduate. I know that it sounds harsh, but don't ever do that again," Conkley said.

Shalum morosely left Conkley's office. As he walked back to his post, he thought about his options. He could talk with the library director, but the rules, he wisely suspected, emanated from his office. He could enlist the senator's aid, but that ultimately would be counterproductive. He could spend seven years attending school to earn the required degrees, but since he already was adept at legal matters, that would be a foolish waste of time. Or, of course, he could just continue with his clerical and paging duties. None of the options looked very promising.

1. Why does this problem exist? How widespread do you think it is?
2. Does this rule always protect patrons, or is it so hard and fast to protect the profession and its members?
3. Do you suppose that jealousy and territoriality play a role here?
4. If you were a liberal (or radical) director, what changes could you implement?

CASE STUDY

Things were not going well for Erin Lavalle, who recently had assumed her duties as head of Information and Referral Services at a large southern university. She had been induced to leave her former position by an increase in salary, rank, and prestige, but she missed her old friends, and discovered to her dismay that some of her new colleagues were abysmally incompetent.

In her new position she supervised eight professional librarians: Two were bright, diligent, and committed to their jobs; four did acceptable work; two were totally incompetent and wreaked havoc, particularly in their dealings with the public. One was a tenured full professor with an astonishing amount of power in the library as well as in the faculty senate, where he had served for 17 years. Lavalle realized that there was nothing she could do here. Roberta Finzyk was another matter. Her inability to do a decent job, follow instructions, learn from suggestions, or deal effectively with the public was scandalous. After six months in her new position, Lavalle broached the possibility of firing Finzyk to the dean of libraries. He, however, was vehemently against this. He explained to Lavalle that despite her poor evaluations, Finzyk would probably be given tenure in about a year. Firing was out of the question. Not only did it raise all kinds of serious problems, but the administration was extremely fearful of another discrimination suit. The last one, settled only the preceding year, had cost the university almost a million dollars in court costs, lawyers' fees, and settlement payments.

Some weeks after this depressing meeting, Finzyk bounced into Lavalle's office. She explained in a long and detailed conversation that she knew that she had been doing a poor job, but that this was entirely the result of having to deal with business, history, geography, and other mundane subjects. Now she had the opportunity to move to Boston and become the theater librarian at a wonderful school. She felt confident that she could get this job, based on her excellent academic record, her three years as a semiprofessional actress, and her vast knowledge of theater history. It was the position she had been waiting for ever since she had earned her M.L.S. All she needed was a strong recommendation from her supervisor. Lavalle immediately balked. "How can I recommend you, when your performance during my entire tenure here has been so dismal?" she said.

"But I just explained that I *could* do a great job, and I will in this new position," Finzyk said. "I just do not like my assignment here. Once I leave, I will become a credit to the profession, and you will be able to hire a specialist for business and history—one who will help to make I & R a much better department."

Lavalle suddenly realized that all of this was probably true, and that this was the perfect solution to a major problem. All she had to do was strongly recommend Finzyk for the theater job.

Lavalle spent part of the next morning speaking with a number of administrators concerning Finzyk's performance in her early days, reading her personnel file, and ruminating. Lavalle discovered that during her first two years, Finzyk had done commendable work, and despite her recent performance, people liked her. "So," Lavalle thought, "it really would not be dishonest to praise her for those accomplishments. It really would not stretch the truth to recommend her for a position that she certainly could fill competently. Yes, it would be okay."

1. Would it?
2. Is it ethically acceptable to achieve positive ends using negative means?
3. What is the harm, if Finzyk does turn out to be a superb theater librarian?
4. Is such purposeful deception ever professionally acceptable? (Consider other areas; e.g., medicine and law.) Why? Why not?

Chapter 3
Selection and Technical Services

Technical services incorporates a wide range of tasks, including selection,* acquisitions, ordering, recording, cataloging, classifying, and maintaining a traditional or online catalog. In a small public library, one person would likely be responsible for all of these activities (and a host of others). In a large university collection, 10 or more professionals plus paraprofessionals and students might be involved. Despite the great variation in numbers of personnel, the opportunities for unethical actions remain fairly constant. The gamut of possibilities is, of course, not as broad as it is in medicine or law, but there are a surprising number of areas in which ethical considerations can play an important role. This is especially true today for two reasons. First, many unquestioned and acceptable practices of the past are no longer tolerated, e.g., receiving gifts in exchange for favoritism. And second, it is my opinion that the immoral climate that has evolved in the United States since the Watergate scandal has led to such a plethora of unsavory events—including the Iran/Contra scandal, allegations of impropriety against more than 100 people associated with the Reagan administration, stock market collusion, falsification of business records, and legal and medical malfeasance—that many commentators are calling for dramatic reforms. This attitude is slowly being adopted by those in librarianship. Thus, what might have appeared acceptable or even harmless in the past could now be grounds for strict censure or even dismissal.

---

*Selection and collection development may be done by technical-service personnel, reference librarians, general staff members, or bibliographers. It is only for convenience that it is noted here.

SELECTION

The selection of library materials, including books, serials, periodicals, and all forms of media—e.g., filmstrips, slides, videos, recordings, cassettes, and maps—appears, at first glance, to be an innocuous activity. The process itself takes many forms, depending on the type of library and the philosophy under which the selector operates. But whether the material is culled from brochures, professional reviews, or approval plans, the choice is made based upon some set of criteria appropriate to the situation. Public libraries, for example, have to consider durability, whereas that criterion is much less important in a specialized industrial collection, where the volume is used briefly and then replaced by a newer edition.

The most obvious ethical problem for selectors is avoiding various forms of censorship, and this is discussed in chapter 7. Judicious selection and collection development requires one to avoid outside pressure. Suggestions, especially in special and university settings, play an important role, but sometimes suggestions can be motivated by a researcher's personal interest or a faculty member's misguided attempt to develop an inappropriate or expensive area. If this is the case, it is up to the selector or bibliographer to explain why it would be inappropriate to order the material and, ultimately, to refuse to cooperate.

Failure to take a stand (often because librarians operate under a severe service ethic and are terrified to say no or to be accused of censorship) or capitulating to unreasonable pressure—out of fear of offending or simply because it is more convenient to spend the hundred or thousand dollars than to alienate a client, a faculty member, or even a whole department—is to act irresponsibly and unprofessionally. The ultimate result is an unbalanced and mismanaged collection. In the case where academic departments are allocated monies to spend as they choose, but consistently purchase inappropriate material, it is incumbent upon the selector to suggest changes, as difficult as this might be politically.

Publishers and vendors can exert extraordinary pressure in the form of avalanches of brochures, advertisements, phone calls, encomiums, and incentives for "invaluable" or "mandatory" but expensive multivolume or microform sets. Frequently, the material *is* invaluable, but if for legitimate budgetary reasons the selector does not think that the library can purchase it, he or she must not succumb to the external pressure. In public and school libraries (where money may be extremely tight), legitimate but peripheral suggestions might have to be ignored. The hue and cry that might follow from individuals or groups is regrettable, but absolute satisfaction and good publicity are only two of many factors that must be considered.

One of the key considerations in selection is the cost of the item. There is no doubt that subsidized university presses can publish books and journals at a cost considerably below that of commercial companies. Large popular publishers have a similar advantage over smaller scholarly presses. Be that as it may, many publishers, regardless of size or interest, price their products in an unfair manner.

Publishers abuse libraries in three ways. First, journal subscriptions to libraries are sometimes two or three times as expensive as they are for individuals. Occasionally, a journal is so exorbitantly priced that, despite its importance, it should be avoided. If enough librarians bring pressure to bear, the price will come down or the publication will cease. The same material will then appear in other periodicals. (Despite the publishing community's double standard and the outlandish library subscription costs, it is certainly unethical to have individuals subscribe and then have them pass the journal along to the library. Such a gift should not be accepted even if there is no collusion involved, i.e., if it is merely an innocent and generous gesture on the part of a private subscriber. A second misdeed only compounds a bad situation.)

Second, publishers price specialized material, aimed directly at libraries, at disturbingly high prices. Some of the Oxford University Press's variorum novel series are an example. These finely edited volumes of Smollett or Dickens can run close to $100 each. These publishers presumably know that college and university collections must purchase these ongoing sets, and they seem to take advantage of necessity. This is egregious opportunism.

Third, European publishers are pressing on with their campaign of multiple-pricing. Books and journals for their own markets are reasonably priced, but these same items, when sold in the United States, carry highly inflated prices which have nothing to do with monetary exchange rates. It is simply that Europeans believe that American libraries can and therefore should pay more. Individuals, networks, and consortia must fight back. Many publishers prosper because of libraries. They should learn to respect the source of their success.

The judicious selector must refuse to purchase overpriced materials and, when possible, attempt to influence other potential purchasers, individually or through networks, to do likewise.

For almost 10 years, and long before it became popular through Herbert White's advocacy, I have fought a losing battle against unfair, discriminatory, and multiple-pricing practices—all aimed at taking advantage of libraries. Here, of course, the unethical activity is initiated by an external entity, but for the librarian to compromise and purchase outlandishly priced items only encourages, aids, and abets such practices.

Additionally, selectors, especially those working with reference collections, must guard diligently against expensive repackagings of the same information. These are easily produced and reproduced ad infinitum from master computer listings by otherwise excellent and legitimate publishing houses. Many of the duplications have a place in large reference collections, but the selector working with a limited budget does not want to spend $300 on material already in the collection under different covers. To avoid such duplication, careful scrutiny of comparative reviews is mandatory.

Selection boils down to choosing from among a large number of sometimes equally useful items. Building an excellent collection in a public, academic, or special library demands carefully balanced work. Sometimes, in large universities, for example, it is impossible to read reviews for each of the thousands of books that arrive on approval plans every month. Nevertheless, judicious choices can be made, despite the lack of time and the large number of items involved. By considering collection integrity and needs, building toward strengths, using a tenable set of criteria for guidance, and abjuring personal preferences, selectors can succeed in creating outstanding collections.

ACQUISITIONS

Much of the work done in acquisitions is of a purely clerical nature, and paraprofessionals or students are usually responsible for typing, ordering, maintaining records, unpacking, and corresponding with vendors or publishers. In a small library, where there are only a few employees, there will be little opportunity for loss. In a large university setting, where tens of thousands of items pass through acquisitions, it is mandatory to impress upon workers the need to protect the material. Employees may attempt to borrow new books before they are cataloged or stripped (for electronic protection); others may actually attempt to steal. Professors and students may wander through and pick things up. Because some items are only in the library temporarily (on approval) and others have been purchased but neither cataloged nor stripped, it is imperative to monitor carefully and protect all materials in acquisitions. There may be more loss there than in most other areas.

The primary ethical problem in acquisitions is probably unfair influencing. In libraries in which choices concerning vendor contracts or approval plans are made by committee, collusion is generally excluded. But when an individual acquisitions librarian makes the decision, he or she may come under extraordinary pressure to choose not wisely but profitably. Temptations may include something innocuous, such as the traditional business lunch, or blatant bribery in the form of gifts or money. There is no way to ascertain how pervasive this type of influence peddling is, but vendors, approval plan companies, and their representatives stand to make considerable sums of money. It is logical to conclude that where unethical activity is possible, it may occur. This is true in every profession, and it is all the more disturbing, because the literature indicates that many people do not perceive such activity as unethical (Kanner, 28).

CATALOGING

One might assume that there is not much room for unethical action in the cataloging and classifying of library materials, this is basically a correct assumption. There is, however, one major area in which ethical considerations do play a role. The people who are responsible for the construction of subject headings and classification schemes are prone to the same biases as the general population. Therefore, prejudicial structuring—blatant and subtle—is built into the Dewey Decimal and the Library of Congress Classifications as well as into the official subject headings lists. Nationalism, sexism, racism, ageism, and homophobia have all been implicitly condoned by the organization of or the language used in these tools.

The importance of all of this for individual catalogers is clear. If no one notes distortions, complains about offensive terms, or attempts to improve matters, then the status quo will prevail. Catalogers come into contact with this material daily, and it is up to them to point out the deficiencies. Hennepin County (MN) Library Head Cataloger Sanford Berman has been doing so for years. For example, when the nineteenth edition of the *Dewey Decimal Classification* appeared in 1979, he found it so wanting that he suggested that it be recalled. Among other problems, he cited the totally inadequate coverage of gay/lesbian matters and popular music as well as the new *optional* use of the traditional numbers for North American Indians (178, 179, 180) which would result in shelving the materials in different locations. In 1983, Celeste West criticized the San Francisco Public Library for using the heading "Literature, Immoral," while failing to provide the heading "Anti-Nuclear Movement." Even if diligent selectors go out of their way to purchase alternative or controversial material, it will do patrons little good if it is lost in the labyrinths of a poorly constructed catalog. (1652, 1653) A careful scrutiny of catalogs across the country would probably turn up hundreds of similar situations.

Another problem arises in the case of cooperative cataloging. Since thousands of other institutions and individual searchers may ultimately make use of one library's cataloging contribution to a network such as OCLC, it is incumbent upon catalogers to produce error-free copy. It is equally important for anyone who spots a mistake to report it immediately. If everyone takes the attitude that someone else already has noted the error, then it will probably remain uncorrected. Original catalogers and stringent adherents of Library of Congress-produced cataloging sometimes find it psychologically difficult to make changes or corrections, and instead go out of their way to defend blatant misreadings or misconceptions. This unwarranted attitude only results in the propagation of misinformation.

A third difficulty concerns copy cataloging. If an institution consistently picks up the cataloging of other libraries without ever making contributions to a shared data base such as OCLC, it is really taking advantage of the other members. Reasons for this type of behavior are varied and include lack of time, funds, or initiative. Very small collections would probably have little opportunity to contribute, but even large research institutions that are hundreds of thousands of items behind in their cataloging (this does occur) would only be forced to do original cataloging on unusual or unique items. It nevertheless would be unethical to consistently make use of member cataloging without ever contributing any.

CASE STUDY

After much controversy, a large municipal library decided to accept as a gift a substantial and fine collection of South African historical, political, and literary materials. The controversy, of course, revolved around the political implications of maintaining a special collection that might, at least implicitly, indicate approbation of the apartheid policy of the South African government. The director and about half of the professional staff convinced the other personnel as well as many of the library's patrons that the collection would help people understand South Africa's inhabitants and ultimately could help that strife-torn country rid itself of an evil political system.

When the complete collection arrived, it was examined by the gift's assessor, who decided that virtually all of the 800 books, 115 pamphlets, and 22 runs of journals should be retained. The material was sent to technical services for processing. Because many of the items were unique in the United States, there were no OCLC records available, and original cataloging was frequently necessary. Will Trenner was assigned to this task. As he progressed with the work, he began to notice that the classifications and subject headings for the historical events that concerned the early white settlers and their progeny were full and detailed, but those for the events of the indigenous population were sparse and often misleading. The extensiveness of the disparity became so evident that Trenner decided to have a talk with Mildred Winson, the head of technical services for the entire municipal system. He described what he had discovered and indicated his great distaste for the official classes (supplied to Dewey by SAILIS, the South African Library Association). Winson was sympathetic, but naturally indicated that there was nothing that she could do about official classifications of subject headings. She suggested that he simply do the best job that he could, so that the library could begin to make the collection available to the public.

Trenner, who had never really cared for political activism, did as he was bidden, but the problem continued to irk him. He mentioned it in a letter to an old friend, who suggested that he write to a leading cataloging activist. His lengthy response was eye-opening. Trenner discovered that other people cared about these misleading classes and headings as well.

In 1986, Trenner attended the annual ALA conference and was instrumental in having the ALA adopt a resolution imploring Forest Press (the publisher of the *Dewey Decimal Classification*) to revise the Dewey scheme to more fairly reflect the history of all South Africans.

1. Should catalogers concern themselves with the political implications of classification schemes and subject headings?
2. Should they allow these concerns to affect their work, e.g., should they refuse to use racist headings? Should they create new headings?
3. Does a local library have the ethical right to arbitrarily create new classification categories or to change headings to suit its own purposes, beliefs, or prejudices? Wouldn't this lead to bibliographic anarchy? Do you think that some libraries do this?
4. If you are sympathetic to Trenner's plight, all of this may appear in a positive light. What if Trenner had objected to some headings that you do not find offensive?

CASE STUDY

Everyone always told Nicholas Frenter that he should have been a lawyer. His overriding concern in every situation invariably seemed to be justice. And he was such a strong-willed person that he staunchly defended his principles and beliefs regardless of the consequences.

For two years, he had done such outstanding work as a selector at a small, private college that he was recommended anonymously for a bibliographer's position at an excellent state university. He applied, was offered the job, and accepted it. His collection development responsibilities included physics, astronomy, chemistry, and geology. Since he had training in all four of these areas plus a master's degree in physics, he was admirably suited to develop the university's nonbiological science collections.

After almost a year, he began to discuss programs and priorities with chairpersons and examine the collection's supporting materials. He was upset by the consistently high cost of periodical subscriptions. He was especially annoyed that even tangential and esoteric journals were priced exorbitantly. He decided to initiate some judicious cancellations, a decision he discussed with the head of collection development. She was rather noncommittal, although she did imply that his project was certainly worth pursuing.

He began by creating a master list of the appropriate periodicals. He read the entries for those included in *Magazines for Libraries*, examined a few issues of each journal, and composed a second list of titles for possible cancellation. With this in hand, he approached departmental chairpersons and explained his position. In each case, he met with strong resistance to the cancellation of even a single title. The chairpersons indicated that they would take up the issue with their respective departmental library committees. Within a month, Frenter received notification that none of the departments would sanction the cancellation of any of the suggested titles, despite the fact that some did not support any program and others were extraordinarily expensive.

Frenter was dismayed but not deterred. He reviewed his cancellation list, chose a few of the most glaring examples, (a communication on mathematical physics and a journal on chromatography), discussed his intentions with the head of collection development, and cancelled the subscriptions. He notified the departments, received some negative responses, and returned to his normal duties.

Almost a year later, when the previous subscriptions lapsed, Frenter began to get some nasty calls and notes from faculty members, none of whom he had ever seen in the library. There were two major complaints. First, he had cancelled the key journal in a person's research area (a statement he simply did not believe). Second, three professors claimed to have forthcoming articles in cancelled periodicals and now their colleagues would not be able to go to the library and stumble upon the essays during the course of normal browsing. Frenter suggested supplying colleagues with offprints or a bibliographic citation through which a copy could be obtained on interlibrary loan. These comments were invariably met with stony silence. Frenter defended his decisions.

The complaints soon reached the higher authorities. The head of collection development and her supervisor, the director of public services, called Frenter in for a meeting. They asked him to reconsider, since the situation was creating such bad publicity. But Frenter insisted that in a period of budgetary constraints, it was foolish to waste almost $10,000 on a few basically useless periodicals. The two administrators agreed, but cited secondary considerations. Frenter, however, stood firm. He had a will of steel and would not yield, since he knew he was right.

1. Are Frenter's actions defensible? Is he wise to be so adamant?
2. Are there sometimes other considerations besides mere cost or usefulness of materials?
3. What should he do if he is *ordered* to reinstate the subscriptions?

Chapter 4
Access Services

Access services may oversee circulation, reserve, and interlibrary loan. For the sake of convenience, special collections and rare books as well as archives are also included here.

CIRCULATION

Circulation must contend with the levying and collection of fines. The demand for any kind of payment generally runs counter to American library philosophy. An exception always has been made for fines, since no really viable alternative has been discovered to coerce patrons into returning materials on time. The collection of monies is an especial anathema to public librarians, who often serve financially divergent populations. The well-to-do have little trouble paying a three- or four-dollar fine, but even such a small sum can be quite deleterious to the very poor, who perhaps need the library's services even more than the educated, middle-class. Academic libraries have to control the use of material that is in great demand for short periods of time, a situation exacerbated when the items are placed on reserve by an instructor. Thus, the fines levied in colleges and universities can be extremely high—five dollars per week for regular materials or a dollar an hour for reserve items. Students who fail to comply with the rules can lose more than library privileges. Transcripts can be withheld and future registration denied. Uncooperative professors (those who have created private collections from the library's resources, and who refuse to return them) can be importuned, threatened, or harassed, but tenure is not usually denied nor salaries garnisheed because overdue books are not returned.

Libraries must enforce the prompt return of materials, but the levying of fines, despite its ubiquitousness, is a questionable method. It does not actually bring the materials in any sooner than the borrower chooses to return them, and it discriminates against those in precarious financial circumstances. During the mid-seventies, after a new computerized circulation system was installed in the State University of New York at Albany library, fines were automatically generated and mailed to patrons, but the money was not actually collected. It would be interesting to compare the return rate under this unusual system with its more traditional predecessor. One possible alternative to fining uncooperative patrons is the philosophical ideal of inculcating a sense of responsibility in each patron. This is easier to accomplish in a small public library than in a massive university system, but it could be attempted. Those patrons who refuse to cooperate would simply lose all library privileges.

The primary ethical problem in circulation is the protection of confidentiality. Patrons often innocently request the identity of those who have material checked out, not to harass or prosecute, but simply to track down whatever they need and retrieve it. In a less ethics-conscious era, it might have been acceptable to divulge such information. Now it virtually never is, and many librarians have fought long, hard battles to protect the patron's identity.* Some 15 years ago, a government agent had the following exchange with a librarian who refused to divulge the identities of people who had checked out books on explosives or subversive activity:

> I happen to be an old-fashioned librarian and...anyone coming in the door of a library I am in charge of can read what he wants in privacy. He shouted: "Do you mean to tell me that you would allow patrons to use militant and subversive material at this library toward the purpose of overthrowing the government?" I refused to answer. I told him that was as if I asked him whether he had stopped beating his wife. He was livid when he left, and I was too. (Cleghorn passim)

Thirty-two states now require a court order for libraries to divulge patrons' identities. That is precisely what Marie Bruce requested in 1984, when a secret service agent and an Oneonta, New York, city detective demanded the name of the only person to have checked out a book in whose margin was discovered a death threat to President Reagan. They confiscated the book, harassed Bruce, and subsequently had the mayor and other city officials bring pressure to bear upon this public library director. But until a court order was issued, she continued to refuse to reveal the person's name. Ultimately, she did comply with a subpoena, and the borrower admitted writing the threat. (Geer) More recently,

> a subpoena prompted Stephen Roberts, Associate Director at SUNY-Buffalo Libraries, to turn over requested records to the FBI, after initial resistance. The FBI wanted the records to attempt to connect database searches with actions of a foreign student they had

---

*Parents may have the right to know what library materials their minor children have checked out.

reason to believe would endanger national security. Buffalo uses a form that requests information about the search; the FBI apparently found the student's copy and wanted to see the key words used. They [SUNY personnel] are now considering ways of dissociating names with computer search records. ("FBI," 15)

What all of this seems to indicate is that patron confidentiality is inviolable, unless someone manages to convince a judge that a pressing necessity supersedes the professional duty to protect an individual's privacy. Traditionally, of course, doctors, lawyers, and clergy never breach confidentiality. Presidential death threats notwithstanding, information acquired, for example, in priestly confession is sacrosanct. Journalists go to jail rather than reveal sources. This commentary is not a call to civil disobedience, but rather an adjuration to consider the individual problem in its context and to react in an ethical way.

Circulation personnel have to guard against favoritism. This is not difficult to do in the public library setting, where most of the clients have equal clout. But in a special library, an insistent or tyrannical vice president's request for material might take precedence over a lowly technician's. The same situation obtains in an academic setting, where a powerful professor's needs are often seen as being more important than a mere freshman's. This is especially the case if the instructor indicates that his or her earth-shattering research depends on the immediate retrieval of the material. Fairness demands that each patron be treated in the same way (within the hierarchical regulations that do allow, for example, instructors to check books out for much longer periods than students). Others might argue, citing triage, that all people, in certain situations, are not equal, and they thus deserve different treatment. But this would be a misleading approach here, since librarians do not deal with life-threatening situations.

RESERVE MATERIALS

The efficient administration of a reserve section, even in a small college library, requires careful attention. At a large university, this is an extremely delicate task. Reserve units are usually staffed by students. This is certainly the case during evening and night hours, when most students do their studying. The material placed on reserve by instructors is presumably the most critical for the course. There is always an atmosphere of tension surrounding the need to retrieve these books or articles, find them unvandalized, and hold on to them long enough to read and assimilate the information without incurring large fines because of late returns. It is mandatory in this situation for librarians, staff, and student workers to be understanding and compassionate. The inflexible enforcement of rules and regulations here only causes unnecessary stress and inculcates in students a distaste for libraries generally.

INTERLIBRARY LOAN

In recent years, interlibrary loan (ILL) has grown to such an extent that it is now one of the most important services offered in many libraries. ILL functions are governed by their own code of regulations. As in so many professional cases, there sometimes appears to be more concern for the profession and its allies than for the client.

One of the most frustrating examples of this is the rule that disallows photocopying from a journal that has been requested by an institution five times within a one-year period. The reasoning behind this is clear: If a library requires a journal so frequently, then it should subscribe. The problem is that even medium or large collections cannot afford to subscribe to all of the journals that ideally would preclude ILL photocopying. It often occurs that a heretofore unimportant periodical publishes significant material which is then cited, and thus researchers simultaneously require it for their work. Once this period passes, the journal relapses into deserved obscurity.

A second scenario depicts a particular project assigned to a large group of students—e.g., marketing typewriters in Kenya—and this very topic is carefully scrutinized in a special issue of an otherwise useless periodical. Naturally, all of the 200 involved students want to see this piece, since the success of their projects and thus their grades depend on the breadth and depth of their research. Limiting access to this essay to the first five requests is capricious, arbitrary, overly protective of publishers' rights, and, presumably, the result of the stringent 1978 copyright law.

When this law first came into force, librarians were extremely timorous about any form of copying. Machines for public use were adorned with warnings and threats that copying was done at the individual's own risk, and that failure to comply with the law could lead to large fines and even imprisonment. Subsequently, the law appeared to be more lenient than originally had been thought; fair use, especially for educational purposes, allows for all but the most egregious abuse of authors' and publishers' rights. As avowed disseminators of information, librarians should do everything they can to facilitate the free flow of articles through virtually unlimited ILL copying.

A second problem in ILL operations is the recent necessity to charge for books. With the promulgation of Daniel Gore's concept of a no-growth collection and similar, if less drastic, schemes, such as cooperative purchasing within consortia, there can be no real excuse for ILL charges. The basic work of processing requests and retrieving and packaging books (or media items, for that matter) can all be done by students in academic settings and part-timers in public institutions. Thus, the cost per item (including government-subsidized postage) is extremely low. The alternative, purchasing virtually everything one might need, is no longer a viable option. It is therefore inconceivable, despite administrative demands, to charge $10 per transaction, as some universities now do. Few institutions and fewer individuals are capable or willing to pay more for a loan than the item originally cost. A small, reasonable fee (one dollar) could be charged by the lending institution, although free service is preferable. If this were passed on to individual borrowers, it might discourage frivolous or unnecessary requests, but it would not be a great impediment to most people. However, it would undoubtedly diminish the general dissemination of information, which is one of the avowed purposes of the library profession. Thus, these comments should not be construed as advocating ILL charges of any kind. Such charges should be assimilated into the budget (as are the costs of books or computers) and other methods used to discourage the unnecessary use of ILL.

SPECIAL COLLECTIONS

Special collections consist of groups of items, many of which individually may not be worth much but when taken as a group become extremely valuable. Therefore, they require special maintenance and protection. Unique and irreplaccable items (Galileo's personal copy of *The Dialogues* with his own notes in the margins, for example) require strict protection from vandalism or theft. And much older artifacts—papyri and manuscripts such as *Beowulf* or *The Lindisfarne Gospels*—are becoming fragile and easily damaged by light and handling. Therefore, many libraries are no longer allowing even textual scholars to use the originals, but are providing them with superb and expensive facsimiles.

All of this is both comprehensible and defensible, but when protection and preservation become ends in themselves rather than means to usage, the true purpose of collecting is being circumvented. A balance must be struck between caring for the items under the library's jurisdiction and allowing patrons to make legitimate use of them. It is, for example, gratuitously uncooperative to refuse to allow genealogists to do research in certain elitist collections. Indeed, such discrimination amounts to an unethical abuse of entrusted materials.

Because of the nature of special collections and the usual necessity to disallow circulation, patrons may become frustrated. A large popular-culture collection, for example, consisting of science fiction or romances or westerns, is likely restricted to use in a reading room, although the individual works (which a patron would prefer to read leisurely at home) are no more valuable than most of the books in the main collection. The only solution is to allow these items to circulate. Curators, however, undoubtedly would balk at this. Rare books, old and modern manuscripts, letters, journals, and other unique documents may never circulate. At times librarians may even refuse to photocopy such material, not because of copyright infringement, but because the copying process can be damaging.

Curators of rare books and other special collections often specialize in these areas because of an inherent interest in the material. For example, librarians in charge of outstanding music collections may also privately collect musical scores, histories, and memorabilia. This is obviously a dangerous position for them to be in, since they may be tempted to increase their private holdings at the expense of professional commitments. If catalogs of outstanding bargains arrive at work, for example, the librarian could immediately call in private orders. Not only is this not illegal, but the collectors could easily convince themselves that these new scores or books are superfluous or inappropriate for their employers' collections. Thus, through self-deception, conflicts of interest easily can be ignored.

Much worse is the bibliomaniac or dishonest professional who simply steals valuable books, plates, or artifacts for a private collection or for later resale. This, naturally, is blatantly illegal as well as unethical, but the possible loss of prestige and employment compounded by a fine or imprisonment is apparently not sufficient discouragement, because instances of such theft are surprisingly common among patrons, librarians, and even high-level administrators. For example, a former librarian at the University of Oklahoma Libraries was sentenced in 1984 to four years' probation for stealing rare books from the library. In 1986, a university librarian in Boston was arraigned because he was accused of selling some 40 of the library's books for $162,000, which he kept. ("Rare," 19)

The fourth draft of an ALA committee's "Standards for Ethical Conduct for Rare Book, Manuscript, and Special Collections Librarians" contains nine points. It calls for a respect for the privacy of both rare and special book collectors and the persons named in the documents. Appraisals should be made only in accordance with the purposes of the collection. And freelance appraisals and commercial dealing may be carried on only with a supervisor's approval. If these standards seem rather lax, the document's admonition that potential special librarians must "assent to them as a condition of employment" appears somewhat draconian. ("Standards" passim)

ARCHIVES

Archivists collect, preserve, and maintain documents and records in a variety of formats. Unlike printed books, journals, and even manuscripts, archival records are often disparate. A single file drawer, box, or linear foot might contain one individual's correspondence, drafts of essays, journal entries, personal records, and so on. Locating precisely what one needs can be an onerous task for the researcher. Thus, creating comparatively easy access through finding aids is one of the archivist's primary concerns.

Maynard J. Brichford, the president of the Society of American Archivists (1979/1980), suggests that standards or guidelines might not be the most appropriate means of solving archival problems. Instead, "individual archivists must assume a personal responsibility for archival principles, independent of institutional allegiances and responsibilities." He also holds that expensive conservation procedures are not mandated for all items. Careful appraisals and difficult choices are necessary here; as for the rest: "Let them rot," from which follows that some material should be discarded or destroyed. Finally, "Methods of establishing intellectual control" should be reevaluated; mere description should be supplemented by emphasizing provenance, history, and biography. (passim) These are iconoclastic suggestions, especially coming from an archival leader, but they are judicious and useful.

Brichford's colleagues, however, were unconvinced, since just a few months after this text was published, the same journal reproduced "A Code of Ethics for Archivists." This concise document denounces harmful competition for materials, "unreasonable restrictions on access or use," and invasions of privacy of donors, collection creators, and subjects. In an unusual twist, the code requires archivists to inform researchers that others are working with the same material and, if both scholars are amenable, each is apprised of the other's identity. (414)

Protecting restricted material is perhaps the archivist's (and special collections librarian's) most difficult duty. Historians, biographers, editors of correspondence collections, and even journalists will become unduly frustrated when they come upon a restricted file just where they most need information. For example, the first collection of Hemingway's letters does not contain any correspondence for particular periods, and none to certain people, because of potential embarrassment. I vividly recall a private tour of the Beinicke Rare Book Library at Yale University. In the basement, one filing cabinet drawer among hundreds was sealed and clearly marked, "Alice B. Toklas: Do Not Open."

Unlike librarians, archivists also control who may use the materials. They may ask patrons why they want to peruse certain files. If they are dissatisfied with the answers, if they suspect that the patrons are not serious scholars, they will block access by refusing admittance to the collection (Linowes, 494). Furthermore, according to Jack Clarke,

> It is not unusual for an archival patron to complain bitterly at the curator's desk that there is damaging information about unsavory aspects of his business or personal life in someone else's papers. Citing his right to privacy, he demands that this collection be closed to the public during his lifetime. In a few instances patrons have asked that unflattering remarks be expunged from the official records. (27–28)

The ethical considerations of archivists are obviously more problematic than one at first might suspect.

CASE STUDY

Lennie Kulpon was a responsible and diligent professor of comparative literature at a western university. In grading the research papers from a senior/graduate course in comparative poetics, he discovered one that appeared to be too professionally polished. He felt there was too strong an infusion of Todorov, Genette, and Jakobson, although these critics did not turn up at all in the student's bibliography. Since his own volumes were unavailable, because he already had packed them for his upcoming Fulbright year in Thailand, he decided to stroll over to the library and glance through the volumes. He called up the books he had in mind on the online catalog to locate their call numbers, but discovered in each case that the book had been checked out and was due back at the end of the semester.

Old Professor Kulpon's blood began to circulate with new vigor. He realized that few other regular students or faculty would use these volumes and no other student had cited them. He would have an open-and-shut case if he could ascertain whether his student had checked out the very volumes he suspected. And this, he thought, would be proof enough, even if the plagiarism amounted to mere paraphrase rather than direct quotation.

Off he went to the fifth floor circulation desk, where he found a young student worker eager to assist him. He asked her to tell him the name of the patron who had checked out the three volumes he had in mind. She, however, was astute enough to recall Rule Number 2: "Never divulge the names of patrons. In case of problems, call a supervisor." And that is what she did. Professor Kulpon was surprised by her noncompliance, but he remained confident that a librarian would be able to help.

Marge Albers, the head of access services, soon disillusioned him. She explained that it would be a breach of confidentiality and totally unacceptable professionally to divulge a patron's identity.

"But," he pleaded, "this student is probably guilty of plagiarism, which is a breach of university policy, grounds for failure in the class and, in egregious cases, grounds for dismissal from the university."

Albers, however, stood firm. She had been taught that professionals maintain confidentiality, and this she planned to continue to do. Professor Kulpon was frustrated and angry, and, as he left, he said that he planned to stop by the library director's office.

1. Do you see that there are two professional dictates in conflict here?
2. What would you have done in a similar instance?
3. How would you react, if your director confronted you and insisted that Professor Kulpon had the right to the information?
4. Is there a possible alternative solution to this problem?

CASE STUDY

The Midvale Public Library serves a small but fairly wealthy community in northern New England. It is supported by public funds and has never had any real financial problems. It, of course, provides traditional services, but it also has been responsible for some creative and innovative advances in public librarianship. The ILL section has been activated only infrequently, since the usual patrons have had little need for items not already in the collection.

In June 1984, Dr. Reggie Opers retired after 45 years of university service. He decided to spend most of his time at what had been his summer home, just outside of Midvale. Although he actively published essays and books throughout his career, he long had wanted to devote all of his energy to a full-scale analysis of economic and social changes in Southern China during the nineteenth and twentieth centuries.

Since there is no college or university within a hundred miles of Midvale, Opers began to avail himself of the public library's services. Opers was a pleasantly charming man, and so Roger Brone, the sole professional librarian, did not mind acquiring the various articles and monographs that Opers requested through ILL. Indeed, long ago, Brone had studied on Taiwan, and he was gratified to help Opers and discuss the project with him. This type of intellectual stimulation was rare at the Midvale Public Library, and Brone had suffered accordingly.

About six months after Opers's arrival, a small boarding school for learning-disabled adolescents opened in Midvale. It was well-funded, provided new economic stimulus for the town, and was a socially responsible institution. Most of Midvale's residents were gratified. One instructor had a part-time assignment to help to develop a learning resources center, but this was a slow and tedious process. In the meantime some of the teachers and students required specialized materials available only from large and distant collections.

Suddenly, Brone was inundated by additional ILL requests. He wanted to be helpful and he certainly tried, but it soon became apparent that he had neither the time nor the resources to handle such a plethora of requests. He realized that, ironically, he was allocating a growing percentage of both his time and budget to only two patrons—Opers and the new school. After much soul-searching, he decided to have a talk with Opers, whom he had faithfully served for six months. He explained the problem. Opers was sympathetic, but he still needed much material, since he was just in the early stages of his project.

"I am committed to living in Midvale," he explained, "and even if I could drive the hundred miles to a college library, I am certain that the ILL person would not have your linguistic skills in Chinese. I know that I have been stretching your capacities, but I do not think that I am abusing my rights and privileges. If you stop processing my requests, my project will grind to an immediate halt."

Brone thought about having a similar discussion with the school authorities, but the prospect for a swift solution there did not look good. He thought about consulting with the board of trustees, but he feared that they would make an arbitrary decision and order him to act accordingly. He was slowly sinking into a nonfunctioning depression.

1. Is Opers abusing a privilege?
2. Should the school make a well-stocked library one of its highest priorities?
3. Has Brone been too helpful, or is it his professional commitment to fully serve even in a situation such as this one?
4. What can Brone do to alleviate this problem?

Chapter 5
Reference

Ethical considerations are undoubtedly of greatest moment in reference work. Recently, this traditional area has been expanded in some libraries to include not only the provision of information but also referrals, both within the confines of the collection and to any external person or agency that could help, suggest, or succor. Thus, the information and referral (I & R) specialist sometimes may act more as a counselor than as a traditional reference librarian. These new duties compound the librarian's ethical burden.

INFORMATION PROVISION

Reference work is one of the most immediately useful and satisfying tasks in librarianship. Its avowed purpose is to supply patrons with information that they cannot locate. This is accomplished either through guidance or by actually seeking out the information and presenting it. In special libraries or situations, the service may also include research, organization, typing, and the ongoing selective dissemination of information for particular patrons.

Professional mandates have long held that the nature of the inquiry is irrelevant. The purpose for which the information will be used is not the concern of the librarian, whose sole obligation is to ferret out whatever is requested. John Swan, in fact, insists that the very provision of information is an ethical imperative. (Wiener, 161) Indeed, for Swan, this is the primary obligation in librarianship, and impeding access to information is virtually never condonable. But it is the general contention of this volume that principles, casuistic codes, rules, regulations, and at times even laws cannot control the social interactions of human beings in an absolute way.

There may always occur exceptions to any given imperative, and that is when ethical dilemmas arise. In medicine, "First do no harm" is an excellent dictum, but if a patient has a gangrenous leg, and amputation is equated with harm, so that the doctor refuses to operate, the patient probably will die. Protecting and advancing the free flow of information is commendable, but there may be times when it is ethically unacceptable.

PRIVATE BELIEFS AND PUBLIC SERVICE

Most human beings interact socially according to some set of prescribed rules. These can be explicit (as in religious precepts, a personal moral code, or laws) or implicit within the social ethos for those who give little thought to these matters. In America, since virtually all of these moral imperatives derive ultimately from the Judeo-Christian ethic, through which one learns respect for life and property, many personal beliefs are held ubiquitously. Most people have a general idea of what is right and wrong, despite the fact that in an open and liberal society what is acceptable may be dramatically diverse, and at times even antithetical to each other. There is little doubt that the Foskett/Swan position is usually correct. If the information provider filtered each request through a personal set of criteria, insisting that none of his or her personal beliefs be countered, the result would be professional chaos, since many patrons would be turned away for illegitimate reasons. And as Swan observes, reading about a particular activity is not necessarily the same as performing it. (Wiener, 162) Therefore, the careful and censorious scrutiny of each request in terms of one's beliefs obviously is neither warranted nor advocated.

Conversely, an *absolute* adherence to the dubious professional commitment of dispensing information is also unacceptable. Patrons and their needs are only one factor in a complex social equation that includes librarians, employers, and society generally. For the library professional to consider the patron in a vacuum is analogous to the case of the lawyer who fervently defends an admitted criminal and gets him off on a technicality. The criminal's rights have been protected, but at the expense of both his or her victims and society. What is suggested here is that a professional's primary obligation is to be aware of divergent possibilities, to consider, to think, and to balance the needs of the patron with those of society.

Furthermore, most commentators tirelessly insist that patron wants and patron needs are seldom synonymous. Carrying this somewhat specious observation to one possible conclusion, it might be insisted that clients in search of harmful information, like how to commit suicide (with the intention of attempting it), may not know their real needs, and the librarian could guide and sway them. This, admittedly, is an extreme scenario, but it follows logically from the lack of faith reference personnel place in the typical patron.

Interestingly enough, this very problem is posed in one of the ALA Ethics Committee's questions to the profession, presented from time to time in *American Libraries*: "A reference librarian is asked by a student for a copy of *Suicide Mode d'Emploi* (a French publication linked to 10 suicides). "Do you find him the book? If so, is that all you do?" The seven replies published are a fair demographic representation—sexually, geographically, hierarchically, and typologically. This balanced diversity is rather less remarkable than the multitude of opinions expressed. James Burnett, for example, is hard-nosed in his insistence that "the librarian must provide all the help necessary to meet the student's needs. No other course of action is possible." A second person is just as insistent but rather more humane. Three respondents state that they would dispense the information, but they simultaneously would suggest that the student seek counseling. Another poses a series of counter-questions, the upshot of which is that one should proceed with caution.

But it is Paul B. Wiener who provides the fullest and most balanced approach. He avoids the self-righteous and pontificating defense of professional duties that some of the other respondents manifest. Instead, he indicates that he would act according to the dictates of the situation. He describes a number of possible scenarios and incisively concludes: "The point is, since we're only human, let that be the basis of helping each other, not cut-and-dried 'professional' guidelines that treat information as if all of it belonged in a computer." ("Is it Ethical?", 643) Precisely!

SUSPICIONS, FEARS, AND APODICTA

It is a lamentable fact that librarians have never been overly concerned with the ethical implications of their work. They simply ignore all but the most blatant problems. In the case of reference personnel, it is much easier to unthinkingly provide the information than to wonder, question, cause a brouhaha, be reprimanded, or even risk the loss of one's livelihood.

When faced with a situation in which two ethical commitments pull in opposite directions, the reference librarian must make an immediate decision based on a swift examination of the operative principles. This decision may vary depending on whether the detrimental consequence is merely suspected or ensured. As critics of my position tirelessly point out, patrons require information to make considered choices, reading and acting are not synonymous, and many information needs simply fulfill academic assignments. But occasionally, there *is* a strong hint that the tendered information may lead to harm or even catastrophe. The librarian should hesitate, balk, or even refuse to help, depending on the specific case.

ˉ In the bomb experiment briefly discussed in chapter 1, the author concluded that reference personnel should not have been so overly helpful. They might have questioned the patron's motivation, merely pointed to a useful tool, or even indicated that they could not render assistance. Consider Mary Prokop and Charles R. McClure's examples of impending harm based on tendered information.

> [S]everal hours after John Hinckley attempted to assassinate President Reagan, a woman identifying herself as a journalist called a library and asked for the telephone number of anyone named Hinckley in Ardmore, Oklahoma. The student assistant who took the call found herself wondering whether the caller actually was a journalist, what the purpose of a phone call to the Hinckley family might be, and, if harassment were the result, whether she as the information intermediary would be contributing to the harassment. The conflict between personal and professional ethics is apparent.
>
> [A] prison librarian was approached by an inmate, an admitted neo-Nazi, who requested that several titles dealing with white supremacy be obtained for him. The librarian had a personal antipathy for the subject, and also was reluctant to provide such materials in an atmosphere where an undercurrent of racial tension is always present. Still, she recognized that other inmates received books pertinent to their interests, and she felt that denying this patron's request might amount to discrimination. After wrestling with her conscience, the librarian borrowed the books.* (74)

In both of these cases, the reference person merely suspected imminent harm. Nevertheless, refusal to assist would have been warranted. That assistance was rendered is also acceptable. Ethical dilemmas do not necessarily have correct solutions. The outcome depends on the situation and the people involved, and this is especially so when the detriment is only suspected.

A distinction also must be drawn between the unsavory, the asocial, and even the unethical on the one hand and the blatantly illegal on the other. There is a difference in kind between harassing the Hinckleys or fomenting unrest and abetting or aiding in the commission of major crimes such as murder, terrorism, kidnapping, rape, or armed robbery. In these cases, even mere suspicion demands judicious action and the possible refusal to help the patron, who, of course, can explain that he or she has been misunderstood or misinterpreted if confronted by the librarian. The patron also can visit another library. That is, analogously, precisely what clients do when they are dissatisfied with information tendered by doctors or lawyers: They seek a second opinion.

The preceding discussion focuses on the mere suspicion of socially harmful, unethical, or illegal activity. Prokop and McClure are

---

*These two instances derive from personal interviews conducted by the authors.

devastating in their condemnation of all of this hypothetical conjecturing:

> If librarians recognized that they should be held responsible only for the knowledge they have about the professional base—librarianship—confusion about whether or not it is ethical to dispense types of information would diminish.
>
> Ethical behavior depends upon how well (and how impartially) the librarian provides access to information, not upon the ability to divine possible harmful consequences. (77)

And in a sense they are correct. Librarians are information dispensers, not prophets. At the same time, they are also members of society and owe part of their allegiance to this larger group. Thus, Prokop and McClure are rather unfair in their absolutism.

A very different perspective emerges, however, when mere suspicion is replaced with certitude. Even adamant critics like Swan admit that when the librarian *knows* that the information provided will result in detriment, some forestalling action is demanded. This type of situation obviously occurs only rarely, but when it does, it is incumbent upon the librarian to withhold the information. In such a case, ethical precepts or laws protecting life or property take precedence over the commitment to dispense information.

A hypothetical but by no means unlikely example should help to clarify this: A distraught male approaches the reference desk in a large public or academic library. He has just discovered that his wife has left him and has sought protection from his constant harassment and abuse at a local women's shelter. He needs the addresses of all of the city's shelters. He is raging and ranting that he will kill his wife when he finds her.

In order for a librarian to safely refuse to help, he or she must do three things. First, the librarian must consider the request within an ethical context. Second, a decision must be made that dispensing the information is wrong. And third, the librarian must take precautions to avoid physical harm. Once these three activities have been completed, the librarian might call for assistance, equivocate, or simply turn the patron away. Aiding the deranged husband would be ethically reprehensible and a complete dereliction of one's responsibilities as a human being and as a professional. Women's shelters, by the way, are refuges for battered and abused women and children and generally keep their locations secret. It is, however, possible that a women's almanac or other handy reference tool might foolishly include them.

Finally, it should be noted that the angry, the tormented, the abusive, and the mentally incompetent make use of libraries just as the ordinary citizen does. I once watched a frequently observed madman lose complete control: He removed book after book from the shelf of a large academic reference section and threw them wildly across the floor. He was escorted away by the police.

Situations in which it is known that the provision of information will lead to detriment give rise to a further complication. It is the contention of this volume that librarians must act in such a way that they, and not professional organizations, codes, or employers, are ultimately responsible for their actions. (The Nuremberg defense is never admissible.) But, despite the implication of critics, I have never indicated that anyone is responsible for another person's actions. Furthermore, the general professional imperative to protect confidentiality is always operative.

Thus, if in the course of helping some people, the reference librarian inadvertently discovers that they *are* planning to plant a powerful bomb in a busy post office, he or she is faced with a difficult dilemma: to protect confidentiality or to inform authorities and perhaps save hundreds of lives at the expense of confidentiality. A journalist or a lawyer might not breach the confidence; a confessor priest would not. Following logically, the librarian should not either. I iconoclastically dissent; the protection of human life takes precedence over patrons' confidences; therefore, in this case, I hold that it is ethically preferable to contact the police. In conclusion, it is necessary to insist that the ethically induced refusal to provide information should not be confused with censorship, which is the topic of chapter 7.

CONFLICT OF INTEREST

The wary have to be on constant guard against conflict of interest. This problem usually occurs in professions in which service is rendered for a fee, that is, where bribery, graft, collusion, influence peddling, or secondary interests are probable. But like acquisitions personnel, reference librarians can find themselves in situations in which their actions may be influenced by external interests. Business specialists in public, academic, or special libraries may own small but diverse stock portfolios. They easily could sway a typical, uninformed patron seeking investment advice. This could be done purposely or even unconsciously, since people generally attempt to maintain their own best interests.

Reference librarians, especially in smaller communities where there is less possibility of diversity, may act as external consultants, board members, or trustees, and thus interact financially with potential patrons who might make unwarranted demands on the librarians' professional services. Additionally, with the ubiquitous implementation of database searching and other services for which money is routinely collected, there is always the possibility of monetary malfeasance.

SERVICE: QUALITY AND ACCURACY

Etiquette, including professional courtesy, usually is taken for granted, and this perhaps is an error. Harried, harassed, overworked, or burned-out personnel may be curt, surly, dismissive, or completely unhelpful. A librarian's assiduous concentration on peripheral matters while awaiting patrons may deter certain people from approaching the reference desk. This is often evidenced by those two infamous preambles: "Sorry to interrupt!" and "I have a dumb question." Sometimes personal adjustments are necessary. A hyperactive New Yorker working in the more relaxed atmosphere of a southern library may alienate patrons simply because he or she is overly efficient.

The librarian's professional attitude toward patrons is analogous to a doctor's bedside manner. When the latter is poor, the advice and even the cure may be negatively affected. Precisely the same situation obtains in the reference process. Discourtesy on the part of the librarian can have a detrimental effect on the reference interchange and the information tendered.

The quality of service should be consistently high. It should never be rendered based on the personal characteristics of the patron. Appearance, sex, race, age, authority, or other peripheral matters must never have an effect. Reference personnel should strive to do their best and to present the fullest and most complete answers regardless of tangential influences.

Studies, unobtrusive observations, and personal reflection all indicate, however, that this ideal frequently is not attained. A young, messy bohemian is not as well served as the library trustee or university president. Children are directed to other locations or deterred from reading "inappropriate" material. Members of the opposite sex can receive preferential treatment. A difficult or scary client is hurried through the process. For example, a patron at the Library of Congress requested a picture of the Iron Curtain. Judith Farley, the librarian, tried to explain that this was merely a metaphor, but the patron insisted that it really existed. Because five other clients were waiting for help, Farley shunted the picture seeker off to the card catalog. (14)

Note that there is one area in which preferential treatment is warranted. At times, librarians are called upon to help disabled persons. A simple task for the able-bodied (searching a catalog, reaching for a volume) may be an impossibility for the disabled. In these situations, it is incumbent upon the librarian to render extra service. A blind student once asked me to retrieve a journal. On the way back to the reference desk, I voluntarily made a copy of the article she needed. This saved her the embarrassment of asking a stranger to do so. All in all, there is little doubt that there is substantial room for improvement in the general quality of reference service in virtually all types of libraries.

One of the most controversial areas in reference work is the apparent inability of ostensibly competent personnel to furnish satisfactory answers. David E. House and Marcia J. Myers and Jassim M. Jirjees, among others, have shown that librarians provide inadequate, misleading, or inaccurate information in about half of all cases. This is certainly a dismal showing. Doctors, lawyers, and engineers sometimes fail in their endeavors, but a 50 percent success rate would quickly put these people out of business. So much emphasis is placed on information provision that information accuracy is apparently slighted. The cynical might conclude that as long as free access to information is protected, the information furnished can be irrelevant or incorrect.

The primary cause for this ineptitude must be imputed to education for librarianship, in which procedure is stressed, substantive knowledge in other disciplines is deemed unimportant, and one brief course in reference prepares future librarians for their duties. Furthermore, Samuel Rothstein convincingly argues, the lack of financial aid for maintaining competence through continuing education plus the absence of penalty for shirking such responsibility is an ethical problem of large dimension ("Where," 4), one that is compounded in situations in which the administration actively discourages formal continuing education.

MEDICAL AND LEGAL INFORMATION SERVICE

Perhaps the most subtle ethical problem is learning to distinguish between advice and mere guidance in medical and legal reference work. Questions in these disciplines occur frequently in most public and academic libraries and increase dramatically in collections in hospitals, law offices, and institutions that educate practitioners. For unlicensed personnel without a J.D. or M.D., dispensing information in an advisory or interpretive capacity is not only unethical, it is also illegal, and the librarian could be prosecuted for practicing medicine or law without a license.

In an excellent overview, M. Sandra Wood and Beverly L. Renford point out that general ethical dilemmas in reference are exacerbated in hospital facilities, where doctors require immediate, accurate, and current information to save lives through, for example, diagnosis, detoxification, or unfamiliar surgery (75, 76, 82). (Mutan's mutandis, this would obtain in law offices as well, though to a lesser extent.) A new and complex area is patient education, and here, as Wood and Renford note, the librarian is sometimes asked to withhold information from a patient—e.g., by the attending physician (79, 81)—which is, of course, anathema to the library profession.

Helen Crawford points out that some medical librarians prefer to participate in the normal work that scientific librarianship entails, but feel "uncomfortable with patients and their relatives and with laymen in general, uneasy at intruding upon the doctor-patient relationship, and fearful of doing harm." (336) However, it can be seen that attitudes have changed somewhat since Crawford made this statement.

Many hospitals, especially in the eastern United States, separate their professional collection (open only to medical personnel) from the patient library. However, many patient libraries that previously contained only recreational reading now also include medical materials appropriate for lay persons.

Daphne Pringle, a patient librarian, explained that patient attitudes have changed dramatically since Crawford published her essay: There is now a strong demand for patient health information. Pringle is not uncomfortable working with patients, since that is precisely what her job entails. She is at liberty to dispense certain types of medical information, although some institutions still forbid doing this and thus their patient libraries do not contain medical materials. (Pringle)

A medical reference librarian in a professional collection indicated that she is indeed uncomfortable with patients, has them work through a doctor, and may even refuse to help, but this is because she usually does not deal with patients, whom she can refer to the non-professional library. (Telephone)

At Overlook Hospital (a 600-bed facility) the professional and patient libraries are combined. Librarian Kathy Moeller insists that a strong consumer health collection is mandatory, and so she purchases in this area and advertises her services to the community. She dispenses general information but shuns diagnoses, advice, and comments on a patient's specific condition. If these types of information are requested, she suggests that a doctor be consulted. She is neither uncomfortable with patients nor fearful of doing harm. (Moeller) The past decade compounds the ethical problems for both medical reference and patient librarians.

Legal reference service in a public or academic facility differs markedly from that which is rendered in a law library. The clients in the general collections are lay persons or students with no real expertise in legal matters. Thus, their wants can be simple and they can be satisfied fairly easily, as in the cases of lay persons seeking specific laws or business students who come prepared with correct citations to federal and state legislation or court cases. When these people's needs are more complex, as is often the case in a law library, whose patrons consist of law students, lawyers, professors, legislators, and judges, they cannot be helped because this would entail the practice of law. In such cases, the librarian should suggest that the patron consult an attorney.

Peter C. Schanck observes that general reference librarians are not knowledgeable about the law, nor are their collections particularly extensive (57), and this results in further limitations on service. C. C. Kirkwood and Tim J. Watts indicate that the law librarian's contractual, ethical, and statutory obligations to dispense information are counterbalanced by legal and ethical limitations (68–74). The obligations are basically self-explanatory and do not require further elaboration. Legal impediments to unfettered information dispensing include the prohibition against practicing law without a license and the necessity of serving one's primary constituency, sometimes to the detriment of the general public.

Ethical limitations derive from the legal and dictate that librarians not practice law. A reference interchange does not allow for the calm, confidential, in-depth interview that takes place in a lawyer's office. Thus, patrons may be poorly served and unaware of this, if they solicit legal advice from the librarian and it is given (71–73). Because of these limitations, Kirkwood and Watts insist upon a tactic that would be both inappropriate and unethical in any other type of library:

> The reference interview must be conducted with a view toward determining what information is needed only after the status of the user and the purpose for which he wants the information is determined. The information may be obvious in some instances, but if either the patron's status or intent is unknown it should be found out through diligent and persistent questioning. The burdens of persuasion and proof are on the patron. If answers are not readily forthcoming or are not credible, only the most general information should be provided, including directions. Unless, and until, a patron proves otherwise, he or she should be presumed to be a tertiary patron of the most unstable sort.
>
> The librarian specifically should inquire, as a part of the information-gathering process, whether the person is working on an assignment or is just generally curious. If the answer is the former, the instructor should be discovered. (Not only does this action help prove the patron's veracity, but the librarian may already know what material is required for a particular class.) If the patron indicates it is a matter of general curiosity, he should be referred to popular publications, like *Time* or *Newsweek*. National legal encyclopedias may also be good sources, but state legal encyclopedias are too specific and may contain dangerous references to statutory material. If the patron indicates he is pursuing his case, he should be dealt with as described below.

The librarian must be aware of body language as well as oral communications as a measure of veracity. Mumbling, a lack of eye contact or an unusual air of excitability should be noted. All the senses and experiences of the reference librarian must be used to discover the status of patrons. (75)

This obviously contravenes everything that the ALA, the code, the *Library Bill of Rights*, the *Freedom to Read Statement*, and this book advocate. Dividing patrons into primary users (law school faculty), secondary (law students), and tertiary (lay persons, pro se litigants) and then rendering aid accordingly, in order to protect them from "dangerous references" (74–75), is a bizarre injunction for most information specialists.

Schanck divides legal reference service into a number of useful categories. Providing factual information, pointing to legal tools, and even showing the patron how to use them are all basically acceptable. Interpreting laws and cases, explaining the meanings of terms, giving opinions, and advising on legal matters all constitute the practice of law and are therefore unethical and illegal. (59–63)

Whenever librarians in any type of collection realize that they have reached a point beyond which they cannot legally or ethically venture, they ought to recommend that the patron consult a lawyers' directory, referral service, or community legal clinic. As for an ethical code for law librarians, this appears to be as nonfunctional as its medical analog, since situations vary and casuistic regulations cannot account for the differences. In 1974, a detailed code was prepared and then rejected by the members of the American Association of Law Libraries. A briefer version, however, was accepted some years later. (Schanck, 59)

ANONYMITY

A final comment must be made concerning Joan C. Durrance's contention that librarians are the only service professionals who fail to identify themselves to patrons, and that this anonymity results in flawed communication and protection of the incompetent (Durrance, "Generic" 278, 279). There is certainly some truth to this, but communication will not necessarily be improved simply because reference librarians commence each interchange with a self-introduction or wear name tags. Tags, admittedly, may be useful in a public or special library, but they would alienate many academic librarians who have a difficult enough time maintaining faculty status without setting themselves further apart from their colleagues by wearing badges. As for protection of the incompetent, people can be identified in many ways, even when names are unknown.

CASE STUDY

Joral Epsie is a dynamic intellectual who has fought her way to the top of her profession against seemingly insurmountable odds. She holds an M.L.S. and a Ph.D. and is both head of reference and a functioning reference librarian at a medium-sized university library in Boston. During her 11-year tenure, she has received innumerable compliments on her dedication and work in helping students and faculty, including the selective dissemination of information far beyond her normal professional duties. She is active in two professional organizations and continually publishes substantive essays and reviews. Epsie is also a fervent feminist.

In early August of 1987, a traditionally slow period in academic libraries, Epsie was approached by a young man who asked for help in locating marketing information, including demographics and potential sales, to open a bookstore in one of Boston's suburbs. After some preliminary work and discussion, the patron indicated that the store was to be located in Somerville, which coincidentally is where Epsie happily resides. Off they went to the commercial atlases and buyer's guides. Just as she was about to introduce the young entrepreneur to the exciting world of government documents and census materials, he committed a serious blunder. He stated that his store would exclusively stock pornographic books, magazines, and videos.

Undaunted outwardly, but staggered inwardly, Epsie excused herself and returned to the reference desk. Because she had already shown the patron a number of items, he had much work to do, at least for a while. This gave Epsie some time to contemplate her problem. As a firm believer in the *Library Bill of Rights* and other ALA documents, she knew it was her duty to help the patron in spite of her personal feelings. At the same time, she also felt that pornography was an affront to human dignity and resulted in violence against women. She was agonizing over this dilemma when the patron once again approached the desk.

1. Consider what Epsie should do and why.
2. Is there a correct solution to her problem?
3. Should her decision be based on something more than mere personal belief?

CASE STUDY

On a hot May afternoon, just a few weeks before the end of the semester, a gangling male adolescent approached the reference desk. Ruth Dunsmoor looked up from the copy of *RQ* that she was reading and asked how she could be of service.

The young man said that he had been having a hard time adjusting to life at such a large university. This had been his first year away from home, and he had barcly scrapcd by during the first semester of this, his freshman, year. If he did not improve his grades, he would lose all of his financial aid, alienate his pedestrian and unsympathetic parents, destroy his relationship with his girlfriend, and probably not be able to complete his education.

This lament was followed by a short lull, and so Dunsmoor asked once again what she could do. "Well, that's just it—I need some help with this essay I have to write for my English rhetoric seminar," he said.

Dunsmoor glanced through the five proffered pages and was quite impressed. The student had grasped the concept of determinism well; his definition and examples were so polished that they could have come from *The Encyclopedia of Philosophy.* "This is excellent," she observed. "You will undoubtedly get an A. If you can write like this, I cannot understand why you are having trouble with your grades."

"That's just it," he muttered, "I cannot write like that."

"What do you mean? Isn't this your own work?"

"Of course not. I just copied it out of an encyclopedia that I found over in the B section of the reference collection.

Dunsmoor felt queasy. "Do you plan to hand this in as your own work? If so, that is called plagiarism and you could fail the course or even be tossed out of school."

"Are you going to tell someone about this?" he asked.

"No, but I would strongly advise against handing it in."

"Listen," he said, obviously getting down to brass tacks. "I need help in creating some footnotes for this essay, so that it will appear to be my own work. I have no idea how to do this."

Dunsmoor jumped up, but managed to control her voice. "You what?" she rasped. He repeated his request. "This is very foolish. You could have written your own essay, had you simply applied the same time and effort that you have allocated to this preposterous project."

"Maybe so, but it is too late now. This assignment is due tonight and I must turn it in. Now, will you *please* show me how to write the footnotes?"

"I cannot do that. Plagiarism contravenes the rules of the university. I would be aiding in the commission of an unethical act. Do you understand what I am saying?"

The young student stood straight up, glanced down at Dunsmoor and said, "Of course, I understand. But you *are* the reference librarian, and I need assistance. Isn't it your job to help students?"

"Yes...."

"Then help me."

Dunsmoor reached behind her desk for a copy of the *MLA Handbook*.

1. Do you think that a student would approach a reference librarian for this type of help?
2. Should Dunsmoor have lectured the student?
3. What are the two principles that pull Dunsmoor in opposite directions?
4. Why should she refuse to help?
5. Why shouldn't she refuse?
6. Could she be reprimanded whether she helps or not?
7. What would you do?

Chapter 6
Ubiquitous Computers

Post-industrial society is synonymous with the information age. This era has come about at least in part because of computers and their virtually limitless capacity to store, manipulate, and retrieve data and information, which laboriously can be transformed by human thought processes into useful knowledge. If librarians have not been in the forefront of computer applications, they certainly have not lagged conservatively behind government, business, or the academy.

Once terminals or micros are in place, it is necessary to protect them from vandalism or theft. Some of the equipment not used by the public can be located in closed or locked areas, but some may be publicly accessible even when most personnel are off duty. Public terminals are always available. No matter how secure the installations might be, some determined patron may manage to circumvent all security measures. The hardware can be stolen or vandalized; internal electronic boards (which can cost hundreds of dollars) and expensive software and compact disks can easily be removed; even the paper can be taken. It is mandatory for administrators to adequately protect computer equipment, especially in large, urban environments, where crime may be more prevalent.

The simplest computer application in libraries is the installation of micros in a convenient location for public use. These computers can be used for word processing, games, computations, and so on. This is analogous to the traditional provision of typewriters. No ethical problems will arise as long as adequate protection is provided and individuals do not abuse their rights by not allowing others to use the equipment.

Much more important is the growing trend toward online catalogs. In most cases, the card catalog will no longer be updated. When all retrospective inputting is completed, the traditional catalog may be dismantled. It then becomes necessary for patrons to learn how to use the new system efficiently, or their ability to access information will be greatly impeded.

Most people will attempt to master at least the rudiments of an online catalog. Some patrons, especially those not familiar with computers, may balk. I once observed a 60-year-old man attempt to use the online catalog at the 42nd Street research branch of the New York Public Library. After about a minute, he jumped up and shortly thereafter returned with a librarian in tow. He simply could not get himself to interact alone with this user-friendly system. In such cases it is necessary for library personnel to help, demonstrate, and teach—all with the utmost diligence. The manifestation of impatience or the inability to sympathize with the psychological fears that computers engender could alienate patrons not merely from online catalogs but from libraries as well.

Another (though not especially common) form of computer-patron interaction occurs in those institutions that maintain in-house information systems. Here, self-created indexes or actual information is stored and made accessible through an intermediary or directly to the patron who learns how to access the material. Ethical problems include tampering with or changing the program or information, or general system abuse, all easily solved through careful monitoring.

During the past two have decades many libraries have decided to automate their catalogs and circulation and acquisitions facilities. Administrators and committees not familiar with computers, automation systems, or vendors at times have been harmed by the unscrupulous. Concomitantly, sophisticated library personnel occasionally have taken advantage of outsiders. One of the major problems may have been attitudinal. Despite the high cost of automation, library personnel may have considered this simply another purchase similar to new shelving or furniture, not realizing how complex the interaction between administrators, consultants, and vendors can become, and how this complexity can lead all too easily to highly unethical practices.

In an excellent essay, "Automation and Ethics: A View from the Trenches," Wilson M. Stahl discusses the scope and prevalence of these practices. Because of the complexity of the automation process, libraries frequently hire consultants, many of whom are also honest and diligent librarians or educators. Those consultants who are dishonest may be guilty of collusion by accepting some form of reward in return for recommending a particular vendor's system. The consultants, of course, easily can rationalize this unacceptable practice. Some consultants use the same report for more than one library, which is hardly indicative of conscientious application (54, 56). Even when bidding competitively, vendors can "low-ball," i.e., submit a prospectus for an inadequate system. This is done so that subsequently the library will have to purchase more equipment (presumably from the original seller).

Another unethical vendor practice is to promise hardware that is not available. Stahl recounts the case of a vendor who offered a device that more than five years later still had not been delivered. (55) Joe Matthews suggests that vendors would benefit from "an industrywide code of ethics." (95) Some companies have broken ground by instituting individualized ethical guidelines, e.g.,

> Geac introduced a formal corporate code of conduct that applies to every Geac employee. This code is expressed in a written document that is distributed to all Geac employees and is available upon request from the company. The company requires that all vice-presidents annually certify that all Geac sales staff conform with the overall code every year. (Monahan, 103)

Vendors should not attempt to appropriate a library's database; they must avoid price-fixing; they should give full and complete information and not allow librarians to suffer from naive misconceptions; and finally, the slandering of competitors should be eliminated. These stories only scare librarians, who then decide against automating. (Matthews, 95, 97)

Finally, there are three unethical activities that librarians may practice during automation. First, there is wiring, i.e., creating requirements in such a way that only a preselected vendor can meet them. This may be done because of collusion, but also because the library personnel honestly believe that this particular system best suits their needs. (Stahl, 54) Nevertheless, wiring is unethical because it defeats the purpose of competitive bidding. Second is the astonishing practice of coercing a consultant into recommending the dismissal of an uncooperative library employee. And third, it is not uncommon for administrators to lavish high praise on their new but inadequate systems, so that other libraries will purchase the same equipment, thereby presumably forcing the uncooperative vendor to develop upgraded hardware. (Stahl, 56, 57)

Michael Monahan describes some specific cases in which librarians were guilty of what appear to be unethical practices. The most blatant of these deserves quotation in full:

> Geac responded to the proposal for a medium-sized public library system. Our understanding was that the award was to be made in the "low compliant bid" manner. This means that the vendor supplying the lowest bid meeting the requirements would be awarded the contract.
>
> After the bids were opened and evaluated, Geac was informed that it was the expected winner. This was, as always, subject to successful contract negotiation. The other vendors were also informed of the decision. Geac was invited to come to the library for the contract discussions. When the Geac staff arrived, the first item on the agenda was to inform Geac that another firm had modified its bid and was now the low compliant bidder. Geac was offered the

opportunity to reduce its bid. Geac terminated the discussions immediately; the other firm was then awarded the contract. (104)

Stahl, by the way, in addition to pointing out ethical problems, also offers much good advice on how to avoid them. His essay is mandatory reading for anyone planning to automate.

Once the automation process is completed and the systems are operational, a number of preventable ethical problems can arise. Some circulation systems interface with the online catalog and allow patrons to note the identification numbers of those who have material checked out. This is only one step removed from the patrons' actual identities. A bug in the system, especially in the early transitional stages after the computer is installed, could allow open access to confidential information. Hackers easily can break into an unprotected system. Since online catalogs are accessible from any location via a modem, this can be done at their leisure from their own homes. It is imperative to fully protect against this sort of eventuality. A lackadaisical attitude, one that derides such protection as appropriate only for military or industrial secrets, is a warrant for future trouble.

Along with data, computers generate animosity. Automatic (and perhaps erroneous) recalls and fines cause the patron undue anxiety. It is necessary for circulation personnel to react in a humane way to laments or complaints. It is imperative that humans assume responsibility for problems. They should never allow responsibility to devolve upon an inanimate computer. Nothing was ever solved, and no feelings were ever assuaged, by using computers as excuses for inefficient, foolish, or unfair practices.

Lending and now copying of materials are integral parts of most library operations. Only highly specialized research collections deny the former and balk at the latter. As new media have been collected, lending and even copying have followed naturally. This is the case with recordings, tapes, cassettes, slides, filmstrips, films, videos, and so on. (By law, copying is severely restricted for a few of these.)

Logically, then, the lending and copying of software should follow as well. There are, however, two unusual features here. First, software can be extremely expensive. At the same time, unlike an analogously costly film (now replaced with cheaper videos), software is not at all bulky. It easily can be secreted, stolen, misplaced, or lost. Even in-house usage creates problems. Once the $500 disk is removed from the library, it may never be returned. And this raises the second issue. Copying of software is often strictly prohibited; thus, the library should not make a backup copy unless permission has been granted to do so. Therefore, ironically, a policy that prohibits software circulation may be best.

The problem is exacerbated in the case of the newer noncirculating compact disk-read only memory (CD-ROM), which contains materials such as *Disclosure, ERIC,* or *Psychological Abstracts,* whose subscription prices can run to thousands of dollars. If the disk is stolen, the company usually will not replace it, and patrons will have no access to this information (especially if hard-copy indexes have been cancelled) until the next quarterly update arrives. It is, therefore, mandatory for personnel to take every precaution to protect the collection's software and CD-ROM materials.

DATABASE SEARCHING

Despite the usefulness and necessity of many of the computer applications discussed above, the most visible and important computer use in libraries is fast becoming database searching. It has been available for some 20 years, although in its infancy it was so expensive that most individual patrons could not afford it. On the other hand, as late as 1975 the State University of New York at Albany did not charge patrons for searches.

Things have changed dramatically: Costs have come down, and now one does not require extensive training or instruction to do an excellent search. An adolescent can search on databases available though menu-driven systems like BRS After-Dark.

For hundreds of other databases, a trained searcher is, of course, still required. It is human nature to take offense at innovations that degrade professional expertise. Doctors, for example, would find it intolerable if the typical office visit, including all of the probing, listening, tapping, feeling, and questioning, could be replaced by a computer hookup via electrodes and automated queries. Trained online searchers certainly can do things that the untrained cannot, and on complex or hierarchical databases even they may have trouble. But the distinction usually made between the uninitiated patron and the skilled searcher is grossly exaggerated. Even Donna B. Shaver and her colleagues, in their superb essay, "Ethics for Online Intermediaries," overemphasize the searcher's skills. (passim) Anyone can learn the rudiments of online searching in about 30 minutes and with a bit of practice can achieve excellent results. This viewpoint is not nearly as radical as it may appear to the conservative or untrained, and other searchers have begun to indicate this in the literature. (See, for example, Charles Anderson's 1986 discussion, "The Myth of the Expert Searcher." [passim])

One of the most consistently debated ethical problems in librarianship is the ostensible necessity of charging fees for services. Despite the official ALA stance against this, it is a prevalent practice in most types of collections. The general social detriment is obvious: Those who can afford to pay receive information that those who cannot must forego. The greatest impact is felt in the public library, which serves everyone, but even in the academic setting, a poorer student is at a great disadvantage.

Logically and ethically, all fee charging is unacceptable. Individualized database searching is analogous to the infrequent use of some esoteric chemistry tome, which in essence is purchased exclusively for its few users. Database searching costs should be subsumed within the general collection development budget. Despite this perspective, database searching is now virtually never a free service; only a very limited number of academic and public libraries continue to offer searches without any charge.

There are three basic ways in which the cost is passed along to patrons: They pay a part and the rest is subsidized; they pay the full amount; or they pay the entire cost plus a fee. The third case occurs only in libraries attempting to earn a profit. Many academic libraries practice a nasty form of discrimination: Nonacademic patrons, who have access to virtually all other services, either cannot do computer searches at all or, if they can, are charged at a substantially higher rate than those affiliated with the institution.

Ron Blazek addressed the fee controversy in an extensive overview and survey of Florida libraries. He discovered that of the 57 respondents, 14 provided computer services, and 12 of these charged a fee for them (64). Not surprisingly, public librarians were more frequently against fees of any kind than were their academic counterparts. (71)

The most important factor in the database search is the intermediary's competence. Since basic searching techniques are quite easy to learn, many librarians participate in a simple seminar or elicit brief instructions from colleagues. They then begin to do searches for patrons. Some of what they produce is undoubtedly excellent, and much of the rest is certainly acceptable, but there can be no doubt that novices (as well as the experienced) do provide shoddy, inaccurate, or misleading results.

M. Sandra Wood and Beverly L. Renford insist that a poorly executed search is akin to censorship. (83) And Shaver et al. believe that if the intermediary discovers that a search is flawed after the patron has received the results, it is ethically incumbent upon the searcher to notify the patron and to redo the search at no charge. (241) Competence sometimes can be impeded by a personal bias that favors either computer use over a more appropriate manual index or a specific database or method. (Shaver, 241)

The maintenance of confidentiality is one of the cardinal principles in all professional work, and information practitioners incessantly defend its importance. Ironically, though, when it comes to database searching, the patron's confidences can be breached inadvertently in at least three different ways. First, during the initial interview, most facilities require clients to fill out a form stating their name and needs. This form is often available to general personnel prior to the actual search, and afterward it is retained for some unspecified future use. Thus, anyone with access to the files has access to all of this information. (In some institutions, a copy of the search itself is also kept.) Second, librarians may innocently discuss searches, strategies, and problems without going out of their way to protect the client's identity. In a small community, identities may even be deduced from a patron's needs. As Shaver et al. point out, it is a good idea to request prior permission from the patron, if discussion with others is deemed necessary. (242–243) And third, if the patron's name is used online to identify the search, then the vendor also has access to this confidential material.

This disparity between principle and practice is precisely what Mary K. Isbell and M. Kathleen Cook discovered in their survey of 32 academic libraries in Illinois. Twenty-nine of the respondents required a patron's name on the form and 21 required the subject of the search; 27 retained the material for a year or longer. Nineteen held that it was confidential, yet 30 indicated that the records were available to others; and 19 stated that they informed patrons that others were working on the same topic. (484, 485) Thus the firm, principled stand taken by many circulation librarians apparently is ignored here, due primarily to mere inconvenience. The topic of online confidentiality does present one bizarre twist. Shaver et al. note that because of the nature of a company library, all information is available to both other clients, who are alerted to avoid duplicate research, and to management personnel, who are responsible for all salaries and incurred costs. (239)

Finally, the same ethical precepts apply for regular work and online searching: If librarians suspect that the information will be misused, they should proceed with caution. If they know that detriment is ensured, they must forestall it. It is gratifying that Shaver and her colleagues, despite the fear of censorship, insist that "online searchers in their role as gatekeepers have a heightened responsibility in such situations." (242)

Unlike publishers of manual indexes or general reference tools, database vendors earn their income through frequency of use. Each time a search is performed, the vendor collects a fee, as well as royalties that revert to authors, database producers, or others. Thus, a strict interpretation of copyright law mandates that it is illegal and unethical to download searches that are requested frequently. Nor is it acceptable to retain duplicate hard copies to reuse them, thus avoiding duplicate fees and royalties. This is a particularly onerous problem when one is dealing with an exorbitantly expensive database (say, $50 per page) and indigent clients.

Finally, some librarians may become freelance searchers, especially in rural areas, where competition is negligible. This is obviously a potentially dangerous situation, since freelancers may be tempted to convince library patrons that they can provide better service for a fee in the open market than free in the library. In "The New Ethics," Norman D. Stevens castigates the library profession for generally ignoring the fifth and sixth provisions of the ALA code. His is an implicit condemnation of the conflicts of interest that arise in situations in which one's loyalty is divided between an employer and one's own financial commitments. Further comments on freelancing appear in chapter 9.

CASE STUDY

Dr. Nolan Wimmit, the online search coordinator at a major New York City university, recently completed a complex, expensive, and successful search on agricultural-machinery production and export in the United States, France, and Germany. This was done for a faculty member, and her department covered the $60 cost.

A week later, Wimmit was approached by a senior who needed information on the same topic. This is hardly surprising since professors often require students to work on topics of mutual interest. Additionally, assignments tend to be extremely repetitive so that many students may require precisely the same search. While discussing search strategies, the student indicated that she was having an extremely difficult time getting through her senior year. She was divorced, received no child support from her ex-husband, had to pay for babysitters in addition to normal requirements like rent, food, tuition, and books, and now, dismally, she had just lost her part-time job at a fast-food emporium. She was almost in tears when she finished, and Wimmit did not have the heart to tell her that her unsubsidized search, even in condensed form, would cost at least $30. All he could mutter was that there would be a small charge; he then told her to come back in a few hours, at which time he would have the results for her. (He, of course, preferred to do the search with the patron present, but that appeared to be impossible in this case.)

Wimmit spent the next hour brooding. He could send the student to the professor, who might be willing to share the information. He could give her a copy of the search he had already done (a duplicate was kept on file for a year). He could charge her for the full cost of her search, which would help him to learn to be less sympathetic to others' problems. Or he could pay for the search himself.

1. Is a breach of confidentiality possible here? A subversion of an assignment? Illegal activity? An infringement of copyright?
2. What would you do? Why?

CASE STUDY

After a year of frustrating public library service, Melinda Druda finally found a position that would allow her to practice her specialty. She was hired as an economics librarian at one of the premier universities in the country. Besides an M.L.S., she held a master's degree in economics and indicated to her new employers that she had strong competencies in online searching.

One Friday morning, about a week after she began work, a frantic professor of economics (one often touted for the Nobel Prize) asked her to run immediately a numerical database search. Druda's supervisor, Ralph Brenton, had been planning to do it and then accompany the professor to an international conference that evening, but he had suddenly come down with a very bad case of pneumonia. Druda said that she would help him. They discussed the problem, and Druda ran what turned out to be a fairly uncomplicated search, printed the results, and gave them to the professor, who was gratified with the statistics. He mentioned that the paper he was to present at the conference was basically complete, but that these new statistics, at least upon superficial examination, seemed to confirm a new and controversial theory of international monetary exchange.

The end of the day arrived; Druda went home, spent a leisurely evening with her husband, and went to bed. In the middle of the night, she awoke with a gnawing feeling. Something about the search she had run was bothering her, but she could not quite pinpoint it. It grated on her until she arose at eight and made a special trip to her office to look at her duplicate copy. She glanced through it and immediately spotted her error. After delimiting her primary topic a number of times, she had brought in secondary and tertiary topics, but she had forgotten to use the set symbol. The statistics were therefore different from what they should have been and gave an erroneous impression. It would be more than misleading when the professor cited them at the conference to verify his new theory. He would ultimately be extremely embarrassed and would have to retract some of what he had said. And Druda realized that she was entirely responsible.

Since it was Saturday, the economics department was closed. Druda was not yet acquainted with anyone in the department, so the only viable alternative was to call Brenton, who would know where the conference was being held. Druda could then contact the professor before his afternoon presentation. This, of course, put her in an unflattering position. After just one week at a new job, she had made a potentially catastrophic mistake. She would have to admit it to her supervisor, who would obviously wonder how an experienced and competent searcher could do something so inept.

The answer, of course, was quite simple. Druda had learned to search when working on her M.L.S., and then had honed her skills during the first few months at the public library. Subsequently, she had been reassigned, and during the last six months had done only a handful of simple searches on common databases. She had not felt it necessary to mention all of these details at her interview, since she *was* a competent searcher, although apparently rather rusty. Now she would have to admit all of this. It was a very awkward situation indeed.

1. Was Druda wrong to conceal her recent lack of experience?
2. Is she normally a conscientious person?
3. Should she continue to dissimulate, or must she immediately contact the professor through her supervisor?

Chapter 7
Censorship

"Censorship is pernicious, it is un-American, and it is stupid."

William Kennedy

Ch'in Shih Huang Ti was a lucky man. As emperor of China he was able to burn all books, so that history could begin with him. The Argentinean writer and librarian Jorge Luis Borges must have been impressed by this, because after he published *Inquisitiones*, he decided that it displeased him; he therefore purchased the available copies and burned them. And who can forget the bibliomaniac Peter Kien in Elias Canetti's novel *Auto da Fe*, a madman who ultimately burns his outstanding collection?

If emperors and librarians resort to such blatant censorship, it is hardly surprising that virtually everyone else does as well. Individuals; political, religious, and social groups; organizations; academic institutions; and governments all practice overt and covert forms of censorship. Only the ALA, the American Civil Liberties Union, and pornographers condemn censorship unequivocally. I would add my hesitant voice to that list. Censorship is almost invariably untenable, although the ALA's absolutist stance in the *Intellectual Freedom Manual* is untenable as well.

Much has been written concerning censorship. In this context, it is only necessary to insist that it is an ethical imperative to refuse to practice, condone, or abide any form of censorship. At the same time, censorship must never be confused with the refusal to provide socially detrimental information (in reference), the aiding and abetting of illegal acts, or the judicious selection of materials. Such actions may constitute censorship, but they do not necessarily do so. To insist that they do is to misuse the term in the same way that many well-meaning people misuse "genocide" or "holocaust." The absolutist would undoubtedly claim that this is a semantic quibble, a ploy that allows librarians to dispense information as they see fit. But this is simply untrue. It is precisely such subtle distinctions that are important in judicial proceedings and ethical decision making.

Censorship is the active suppression of books, journals, newspapers, theater pieces, lectures, discussions, radio and television programs, films, art works, etc.—either partially or in their entirety—that are deemed objectionable on moral, political, military, or other grounds. Refusing to search out information on the most effective and easily obtained poison for a psychopath who makes it clear that he plans to put it in a city's reservoir is not censorship. It is not a limitation of freedom of expression. The material is not being suppressed, made unavailable, or destroyed. In fact, the information is readily at hand in most collections and the person can seek it out himself. The librarian is simply not aiding in the commission of a heinous act. Furthermore, despite the breach of confidentiality, the police should be notified.

Censorship can occur prior to, during, or after creation of the material, and the author or artist can be as guilty as the government censor or Moral Majority watchperson. In repressive societies, authors who fail to abide by the censor's dictates have their work changed or do not get published. This is why the nineteenth-century Russian writer Nikolai Gogol and more recent Communist bloc authors have written allegory: Beneath the innocuous surface, a more potent tale can be discovered. Apparently, official censors are not particularly astute, since they often miss the hidden meaning.

Alterations and nonpublication are mild oppressions when contrasted with the severe punishments meted out to "careless" writers. Aleksandr Solzhenitsyn spent many years in a Gulag concentration camp simply because of some acerbic remarks he made concerning Stalin. Even in democracies material can be treated with a heavy hand. During the twenties, thirties, and even later, James Joyce, D. H. Lawrence, and Henry Miller all had difficulty getting their works into the United States. For example, government officials often seized copies of *Ulysses* and destroyed them. Editors bowdlerize books to make them more palatable (to the military, religious, prudish, or to children); feminists rail against pornography; and librarians weed out or refuse to purchase objectionable materials.

Censorship is an evil against which librarians must be on constant guard. If the keepers of books, journals, films, compact disks, and software do not vigilantly defend free expression and intellectual freedom, who will?

SELECTION

People have a right to acquire information. This is guaranteed, at least implicitly, by the Constitution of the United States. But there are those who strongly believe that this information should be proscribed. Thus, censorship is increasing dramatically. The Freedom of Information Act is being subverted. Journalists were not allowed to visit Grenada during the American invasion. Political and religious groups control what is published, especially in school textbooks. Large holding companies dictate what their publishing subsidiaries may produce. Parents and school board members inveigh against assigned material, including classics, contemporary literature, and scientific treatises. Problems arise in teaching the Bible, Dante, Shakespeare, Hawthorne's *Scarlet Letter*, Salinger's *Catcher in the Rye*, and Darwin's theory of evolution.

The crisis is so acute that the National Writers Union held a major conference on censorship in the autumn of 1984. The New York Public Library mounted an extensive exhibition, "Censorship: 500 Years of Conflict," between June and October of the same year. As censorship increases, it becomes more acceptable to the public, thereby making the librarian's task more difficult.

The increased instances of censorship and the difficulties librarians face appear to be fairly clear-cut and obvious. Not so, objects Will Manley, librarianship's most iconoclastic commentator. The battle for free expression has been won (formerly taboo subjects, scandalous language, and pornographic videos are now commonplace); the current brouhaha is, therefore, inexplicable. (32) There *are*, he continues, some difficulties in public and school libraries, but this is basically because virtually everyone practices censorship despite the rhetoric to the contrary. Librarians must admit that often they do not purchase material because of the subject matter or "the mode of expression." Once this is admitted, it becomes acceptable not to buy murder manuals or graphic displays of sodomy. (33)

This cursory summary does not really do justice to Manley's analysis. What he says appears to be true and practicable, at least until one is confronted by Celeste West. Unlike Manley, West refuses to capitulate to the subtle censorship practiced (at times inadvertently) by selectors. Instead, she rages against it, insisting that a greater effort be made to purchase alternative publications. (1652) She cites five controversial titles: a suicide manual, a guide to felonious civil disobedience, an advocacy of pedophilia, gun advice for women, and *Anal Pleasure and Health*. She concludes with the following challenge: "Remember, censorship is an excuse for not having to talk about reality. Are there any of these titles you would not order?" (1653)

One suspects that many selectors would come up with countless excuses to avoid purchasing these volumes. Some would be legitimate (a collection does not require every publication), but some would be mere rationalizations to avoid the inevitable problems that would ensue. There can be little doubt that at times selection is synonymous with censorship. And this applies in primary and secondary school, college, university, public, and perhaps even special libraries. But selection as such is not a form of censorship. Lester Asheim, in his classic 1953 statement, indicates why:

> Selection, then, begins with a presumption in favor of liberty of thought; censorship, with a presumption in favor of thought control. Selection's approach to the book is positive, seeking its values in the book as a book, and in the book as a whole. Censorship's approach is negative, seeking for vulnerable characteristics wherever they can be found—anywhere within the book, or even outside it. Selection seeks to protect the right of the reader to read; censorship seeks to protect—not the right—but the reader himself from the fancied effects of his reading. The selector has faith in the intelligence of the reader; the censor has faith only in his own. (67)

Based upon generally cited criteria, selectors positively seek out items for their collections, choosing specific titles and rejecting those that are inappropriate. A certain percentage of most budgets should be allocated to small and alternative press books and journals. The claim that these will not be read is a weak excuse for nonpurchase. This type of literary, political, and practical material has to be made available to be discovered. (West, 1652)

In large research libraries, but also in any kind of collection, there is often a prejudice against media other than the printed word. Slides, films, recordings, cassettes, and software are begrudgingly collected, spurned, or avoided completely. Since much original information is available only in these other formats, refusing to collect them amounts to a subtle form of censorship. If F. Wilfrid Lancaster's prediction that print media will be obsolete by the year 2000 should turn out to be correct, then in just a little more than a decade, librarians will be dealing exclusively with these currently slighted materials.

One of the major problems of censorship and selection concerns sexually explicit material. But librarians, at least philosophically, do not seem to have much trouble affirming intellectual freedom here. In May 1986, *American Libraries* published four responses to its query, Is it censorship to weed *The Joy of Gay Sex* to protect potential victims of AIDS? The two male and two female respondents were unequivocal in their condemnation: Weeding this volume would indeed constitute censorship. Controversial items, despite their danger, have a necessary place in the collection. ("Censorship," 306) These same liberal-minded people undoubtedly would have no trouble with *Lady Chatterley's Lover,* the Marquis de Sade, or *The Story of O.*

Their tolerance might diminish, however, when faced with blatant pornography—obscene creations that have neither artistic merit nor socially redeeming qualities. The problem is that what is indecent to one person is perfectly acceptable to someone else. The inability to define pornography adequately is compounded by the feminist perspective, which defines it in terms of violence, domination, sensation without emotion, degradation, and sexism. This is all noted in contradistinction to eroticism, which is an expression of love and sex. But the eroticism that might be acceptable to a radical feminist like Andrea Dworkin would be highly offensive to Jerry Falwell and the Moral Majority constituency.

A broad range of sexually explicit material exists. Rape, bondage, and violence against women is assuredly degrading and offensive. But so, too, is censorship, and once one makes a commitment to abjure, eliminate, destroy, or even burn these items (as some feminists have advocated), then it is easy to begin to throw other items into the bonfire. It is necessary to add that despite the vocal feminist advocacy of anti-pornography regulation and legislation, many feminists strongly oppose all forms of censorship. ("Feminism") Dworkin and other well-meaning people may be doing irreparable harm to free expression, intellectual freedom, the publishing industry, booksellers, libraries, individuals, and even the general feminist cause.

Another area that can be problematic is selecting for young children's collections. Preadolescents and sometimes teenagers are immature and intellectually undeveloped. They, therefore, are not able to make judicious decisions concerning the material they read, view, or hear. Furthermore, they are extremely vulnerable because they are curious and impressionable, and the impact that negative material can make upon them may last a lifetime. This reasoning is used by parents, school board members, legislators, and even librarians to justify censorship, especially of sexually explicit items. For example, Judy Blume's books, which are fairly innocuous, have often been the targets of censorship efforts.

Additionally, librarians are adjured to select, collect, and disseminate information without regard to race, sex, and other potential discriminators. Many people have worked hard to eliminate racist and sexist language and attitudes from children's books, and to make multiethnic items more readily available. Thus, a librarian who is asked to purchase racist books for children is placed in a difficult situation. For example, a school librarian working in a small community of people with racial prejudice could be asked to buy titles that convey, for example, virulent neo-Aryanist propaganda. The children's parents want them to be exposed to their parents' beliefs, both at home and at school. To purchase these titles is to help propagate racism; to refuse is to censor.

Judith Serebnick, in a lengthy discussion of self-censorship based on the checklist method, cites a study that seems to indicate that high school library media specialists avoid extremely controversial items; restrict usage, which explicitly condones censorship; and do not necessarily order missing controversial items. (35–36) Although Serebnick's point is that the checklist method produces mixed results, there can be little doubt that whereas censorship is often derided, it is nevertheless ubiquitously practiced.

INTELLECTUAL FREEDOM

The public has a right to free expression, intellectual freedom, and information, but not at the expense of individual privacy, which is also constitutionally protected (through Supreme Court interpretation). That is why even information brokers refuse to seek out surreptitiously information that others are attempting to conceal. For example, they will not plant an employee in a company to ferret out industrial secrets.

Librarians help patrons locate available information through published books and journals, microform and special collections, government documents, archives, online databases, telephone inquiries, and so on. They do not attempt to solicit information that another person is intentionally concealing. The refusal to practice espionage, invasion of privacy, or even mere subterfuge delimits the information that librarians can discover and convey. In other words, free access to information is an ideal. In reality, much that patrons would like to discover is proscribed, even statistics concerning the patrons themselves, such as medical, legal, and credit data.

This is also the case for intellectual freedom. ALA's *Intellectual Freedom Manual* espouses an ideal that is, as Leo N. Flanagan argues in an incisive essay, completely unrealistic. He makes six points that deserve reiteration. First, the right to believe and express *anything* is impractical; e.g., false advertising and false accusations are interdicted. Second, the *Manual* grossly oversimplifies; its advocacy of "any mode of communication" is faulted. "Physical blows, torture, enforced starvation, economic or racial exploitation" are hardly defensible. Third, absolute access to information presents legal obstacles, including the right to privacy and the protection against self-incrimination and coercion. Fourth, it is anti-intellectual to hold that ideas and actions are not related, i.e., to believe that reading detrimental material will not necessarily result in negative activities. Fifth, it is unprofessional to abjure making judgments concerning ideas and information. And finally, he indicts the entire profession:

Most librarians hide behind a definition of intellectual freedom which demands no responsibility, which simply commands them to do nothing. And I would suggest that is because they are fearful of making decisions about materials and people with the low level of substantive knowledge that they possess. (Flanagan passim)

So, ideally, censorship is wrong, barbaric, and indefensible. Free expression, intellectual freedom, and access to information must be protected. But realistically, stringent limits are placed upon all of these principles. It is easy to insist that one should neither censor nor refuse to disseminate information. It is much more difficult to justify the requested purchase of pornographic videos for a primary school or a public library's children's collection, even if one is not personally opposed to these items. They are simply as inappropriate as a manual on metallurgy would be. It is equally easy to defend the patron's right to all information until one discovers that a specific client is planning to build a powerful car bomb and set it off in front of a busy department store. Sometimes human necessities take precedence over professional obligations.

TRUTH AND UNTRUTH

There is a recent and unusual sidelight to all of this. In 1984, the California Library Association cancelled a contract with David McCalden, whose Truth Missions' purpose is to inform people that the Holocaust (which claimed the lives of six million Jews as well as other minorities, including Catholics, Romanies, and gays) has been grossly exaggerated. (Swan, 47, 48)

This prompted John Swan once again to defend free access to information. He insists that the truth of a specific contention is of no relevance to the information professional, who also has a "duty to untruth." (46) That is, librarians must make even utterly false material available to patrons, who will then be able to make up their own minds about the issues. Stifling, silencing, expurgating, or censoring even the patently false message of Truth Missions is unconscionable. Here is Swan's eloquent peroration:

It is our job to provide access not to the truth, but to the fruit of human thought and communication; not to reality, but to multiple representations thereof. Truth and reality must fend for themselves within each of the complicated creatures who uses the materials we have to offer. We can and do learn a great deal from bad ideas and untruths. (51)

It is obvious that a consistent negative attitude toward censorship can result in no other position, but not everyone chooses to be consistent. Patricia Glass Schuman has shown that the neutral stance of libraries is assuredly a myth (252). Noel Peattie specifically affirms this for the McCalden case: "We can, and indeed should, be neutral, in matters of taste or opinion; but not on matters of clearly established fact." (Peattie, "Truth," 14)

In a second essay, Peattie argues that Swan's absolute defense of intellectual freedom in this case is therefore untenable: "He [Swan] confuses disagreement over facts with disagreements over moral judgements, and does not separate lies out from his category of 'untruths.'" He then continues, "Truth cannot simply endure the presence of a lie. It has to fight it and overcome it." (Peattie, "Cardinal," 12, 14) Despite the well-meaning, liberal, and anti-censorship perspective, Peattie's overall argument is not as convincing as Swan's: that it is an ethical imperative that information professionals make all material available and accessible regardless of its truth. Swan's is a position that I would endorse, with one codicil: Responsibility to society in general takes precedence over information dispensing (but not over selection and collection, since these pursuits merely make information available to all library patrons) when a serious detriment is virtually ensured. (Despite the pain and embarrassment caused by McCalden's desire to exhibit his wares at the California Library Association meeting, a *serious detriment* was not probable.) Stifling free expression will not lead circuitously to the truth.

CASE STUDY

It had been a particularly difficult semester for Mary Beth Crunton. The K–12 school media center she directed had suffered damage and loss through a fire that some suspected was caused by arson. Recently, though, things appeared to be improving. The district school board had decided to give the center $10,000, an unprecedented sum, to replace lost material and purchase badly needed media, including videocassettes and new software packages.

A small portion of each year's budget was traditionally allocated to purely recreational items—journals such as *Hot Rod*, adventure novels, and Hollywood films and videos. Part of the grant would be used for this type of material, since Crunton believed that the center had an obligation to provide these items to students. She also thought that popularizations would lure students who otherwise might never enter a library.

Because the grant was so large, Crunton decided to solicit suggestions from faculty and students. The response was gratifying. She began to order things at a feverish pace, taking work home at night and on weekends.

One evening, about halfway through the $10,000, she came across some order cards from a group of high school students whom she knew. They were bright, personable, got good grades, and used the library frequently. There were eight requests, all for slasher films on videocassettes. For some inexplicable reason, these realistic horror films, depicting average, friendly people being violently abused, tortured, and repulsively maimed, appealed to otherwise bright and pleasant youngsters.

Crunton was appalled, not only because her peaceful and pacifistic tendencies found this fare disturbing but also because she fervently believed that censorship was evil and that patrons had the right to the material they requested. As a school media librarian, she had run up against this problem before, but she knew that this time she was really going to have difficulties.

The next morning she called in the three students and tried to ascertain why they thought it necessary to add these reprehensible films to the collection. They explained that they had neither intellectual pretensions concerning film history nor social malevolence. They just liked these films and wanted them in the media center.

All of Crunton's well-wrought arguments failed to sway them. They were pleasant but adamant: "You asked for suggestions, and we gave you ours. Please order at least some of these films. Otherwise we will have no choice but to conclude that you are practicing censorship."

Crunton spent part of the day reading the few reviews she could locate and considering her options. The reviews indicated that the films had no redeeming social value, and furthermore never should have been made. This reinforced her initial reaction. At the same time, she realized that in principle the students' requests were legitimate, if inappropriate. But she often did order inappropriate popularizations. She really did not know what to do.

1. Is it always mandatory to avoid censorship?
2. Can you imagine certain cases in which censorship would be a good choice?
3. Is the rigid adherence to principle always the best course to follow?
4. What do you think Crunton should do?

CASE STUDY

After 10 years as a children's librarian in a small municipal library, Effie Rinner thought that she had encountered every possible problem imaginable. During the summer of 1985, she discovered, to her dismay, that that was not so.

The preceding autumn, a group of five men (all of whom had children) suggested that some specific titles on pedophilia be added to the collection. Rinner, a strong advocate of intellectual freedom and not at all prudish in her personal life, strenuously objected that these books and pamphlets were not appropriate for the children's collection. The men countered that this was precisely the place for these items, since they wanted children rather than adults to read about the subject.

Rinner argued long and hard with these people and herself. The upshot of it all was that she relented, ordered the materials, cataloged them when they arrived, placed them in their proper locations on the shelves, and forced herself to forget about them.

In late May, she was approached by a couple who complained that their nine-year-old son had brought home a pamphlet graphically describing and advocating pedophilia. They were shocked and dismayed that their child had been exposed to such a "heinous and barbaric practice," as they put it. They demanded, as local taxpayers, that the pamphlet and all other similar items be removed immediately from the children's room.

Rinner spent 10 minutes explaining why these items were in the collection, that removing them would constitute blatant censorship, and that as a staunch defender of intellectual freedom, she could not comply with their wishes. She would have continued the explanation, but the couple had had enough. They threatened to go to the director, and stomped out of the office. Rinner knew that she was in for a hard time, but when nothing happened for a few days, she once again put pedophilia out of her mind.

In mid-June, the director of the library, Max Trunley, summoned Rinner to his office. She had been so diligent in repressing the censorship issue that she was surprised when he intoned: "A coalition of local parents came to me this morning complaining about some books in the children's room. Is it true that you recently ordered books that advocate pedophilia?"

Rinner recapitulated the circumstances that led to the purchases and explained why she refused to remove them. Trunley was an excellent administrator, stood behind his employees, and always had defended free expression in philosophical discussions. Thus, Rinner was stunned to hear him admonish: "This is an extremely dangerous situation. These parents are upset and angry. They want the books removed, and they will not let their children come to the library until this is done. They threatened to go to the board, the newspapers, and the courts if necessary. The publicity is going to be horrendous, and this could get quite expensive. Intellectual freedom is fine in principle, but this is reality: The Elm Grove Public Library cannot afford—politically or financially—to contest this. So will you please remove these detestable things?"

"No!" she answered.

"No? Why not, for God's sake?"

"You know perfectly well why not. You are allowing pressing circumstances to override the principles upon which public librarianship is based. You are succumbing to external pressure. I won't. I detest these tracts as much as those parents do, but censorship is not the solution."

Trunley stood up and moved closer to Rinner. "Look, we have worked together for 10 years. We respect each other, and we know what is right. Nevertheless, if you do not remove those volumes, I will have no choice but to fire you."

Rinner felt as if she had been punched in the stomach. "Fire me? For upholding the *Library Bill of Rights?* You can't. You can't do that."

"It isn't a pleasant task, but I can. Believe me, I can."

1. Is intellectual freedom the library's only obligation?
2. Should Rinner have ordered the books in the first place?
3. What could she have done instead?
4. Is Trunley being unfair?
5. What can Rinner do now that she is faced with the impossible dilemma of censoring material or losing her job?
6. Regardless of the outcome, Rinner loses. Why?

Chapter 8
Special Problems

Any organization—small or large, simple or complex—that offers services to the public through its employees is bound to be plagued by problems. This study is concerned with those problems of an ethical nature. Chapter 8 covers a number of these that do not fall conveniently within the volume's other chapters.

ADMINISTRATION

Library administrators should treat employees with respect, fairness, and due process. The trend today is toward unionized shops or participatory management. Even in traditional hierarchical organizations, authoritarian or draconian methods are no longer socially acceptable. Such practices alienate employees, the best of whom will probably change jobs. In large libraries, deans or directors and their subordinates should be willing to objectively adjudicate problems and disputes in the manner of an ombudsman.

In hiring, positions should not be nationally advertised, to fulfill some legal requirement if the administration already has chosen someone. This unethical practice is unfair to other applicants, who make many psychological and physical adjustments when faced with a potential employment change. Affirmative action programs should be practiced in the spirit for which they were instituted and not merely to conform to the legal demands of an affirmative action officer. The point of these programs is not to fulfill federal requirements while circumventing the hiring of minorities.

Employees who require references should be treated according to their merits. It is as unconscionable to damn an outstanding employee whom one does not wish to lose as to recommend a flawed person who belongs elsewhere.

Failing to renew a contract, denying tenure, or firing a professional is a most unpleasant task. When truly necessary, it should be carried out with humane understanding. These types of decisions never should be politically motivated, despite the ostensible importance of political maneuvering in any organization.

In fund raising, administrators should neither offer more in return for donations than they can deliver nor compete directly with the fund-raising activities of the larger organization of which they are a part. For example, an academic library should not attempt to divert funds away from its parent college or university.

In industrial libraries, situations can arise in which researchers may discover damaging, dangerous, or illegal matters. Administrators should never ignore or suppress such information. When this does occur, it may correctly result in whistle blowing on the part of the information specialist. The obligation to dispense information (or loyalty to one's organization) is superseded by a higher responsibility to society in general.

Individuals who act as consultants or paid board members for other organizations, businesses, or networks must be extremely careful to avoid situations in which a conflict of interest can occur. This injunction also applies in cases of large monetary outlays, e.g., in building projects, automated-system installations, and collection purchases. Anyone can order, demand, or bully. Effective administration requires diplomacy, a humane attitude, and a commitment to ordinary and professional ethical precepts.

FEES

There was a time, not too long ago, when the demand upon users for payment was anathema to the library profession. (The ALA still does not approbate the charging of fees.) There were some exceptions—rental books, fines, and dues at private libraries—but these were minimal, and none of them really impeded the general access to information. (Fees for database searches were discussed in chapter 6.) Information brokers charge substantially for their services, but that is to be expected, since they are commercial, not public, service entities. (In some cases, brokers compete directly with the less expensive, subsidized services of public or academic libraries). What is most interesting in this context is that the earlier absolute ethical injunction against fees has slowly eroded due to pragmatic concerns. Now even public librarians have little compunction about requiring payment for services.

One might counter that database searching requires payment, while the traditional indexes, books, and journals remain free. Lamentably, this is no longer always the case. Some public libraries now charge a general circulation fee of, for example, $20 per year to those who do not reside within a given geographical area. Twenty dollars is not much unless one happens not to have it. And interlibrary loan sometimes requires a payment. In any case, what is important here is that the ideal of the free public library no longer exists: Information is power, and to gain power requires financial resources.

One of the great advantages of doing research in New York rather than in Leningrad is that even the humblest person can make instant photocopies of noncirculating material. The wealthy or eccentric may carry their own portable copiers with them, but most patrons depend upon machines installed in the library. This is now a generally required service, and to fail to provide it is unconscionable.

I strongly hold that well-maintained and inexpensive copiers are the greatest deterrent to vandalism and theft of library materials. If pragmatic considerations did not interfere, I would defend free copying services, even in academic libraries, where the demand is so extensive. Since budgetary reality intrudes here, I advocate a five-cent-per-page charge. There is no excuse for charging 10, 15, or 20 cents for copying in any kind of collection. Those libraries that do charge more undoubtedly suffer a higher rate of vandalized journals than their less expensive counterparts.

Gathering information can be a difficult task. Libraries should attempt to alleviate, not increase, frustration. The 42nd Street research branch of the New York Public Library obviously disagrees. Here one will find no self-service copiers. Instead, patrons must fill out a lengthy form for each piece they want copied, and then pay 25 cents per page to have someone do the copying for them.

As for the Copyright Clearing Center, an entity that collects money for articles copied for convenience, why it requires a four-dollar payment for five pages is inexplicable. In any case, theirs is often a one-sided contract: They decree, and copiers are supposed to conform by mailing in their payments.

SPECIALIZED SERVICES

Every library may provide unusual or specialized services—for business, community groups, the disabled, distant patrons, or the noncommitted. Some of these are a matter of choice, but others are now socially mandated. For example, Joan C. Durrance argues that various government agencies often refuse to disseminate information to citizen groups. Therefore, "the public library must assume a role in increasing citizen access to information and thus insure the intellectual freedom of the entire community." (Durrance, "Toward," 51)

Outreach programs at public libraries can benefit the countless people who cannot or will not come to the library. Many of these potential patrons may wish to avail themselves of services or can be induced into doing so. The functionally or completely illiterate, the bedridden, the rural, the homeless, and migrant farmers and their children are among those who benefit from mobile units and other outreach programs. Emmet Davis convincingly argues that libraries are under an ethical obligation to serve everyone equally. This includes the disabled; non-English speakers; the illiterate; and those who prefer other media as well as controversial or alternative materials. As he notes, "There should be no silent refusals by omission." (passim) This is sometimes a difficult task, but the primary point of Davis's essay is that it is possible to serve everyone, and therefore librarians should strive to do so.

GOVERNMENT PROSCRIPTIONS

American democracy paradoxically makes it possible to protect individual privacy while allowing free access to information. The Freedom of Information Act (FOIA) opened the archives of many government agencies to the scrutiny of anyone with a legitimate purpose. Only documents crucial to America's security are barred from the eyes of the inquisitive.

At times, though, administrators may wish to proscribe access to government information. The Reagan administration has attempted to do this by abrogating part of the FOIA (using security as an excuse), by cutting back on its publishing, eliminating some government document bookstores, and shifting some publishing to the private sector. B.J. Kostrewski and Charles Oppenheim point out that the availability of information through database searching makes it easy for governments "to restrict or distort the flow of information to some or all of the public." (281)

Additionally, propaganda and disinformation are a constant menace. Any administration that set out to purposely distort the truth could succeed in some cases. It is incumbent on all Americans, but especially on librarians, to fight against abrogations and restrictions to access, as well as distortions of information, through lobbying and the electoral process.

ACADEMIC ADVANCEMENT

Academic librarians often are expected to conform to general faculty requirements. It is becoming more common for college and university librarians to have second master's degrees and even doctorates, substantive knowledge in one or more areas besides librarianship, and a solid bibliography of publications. Teaching faculty are required to be on campus only a limited number of hours per week. This varies depending on the institution. A full professor at Harvard or Yale has a different schedule than a lecturer at a community college. Nevertheless, in general these professors must spend between 12 and 20 hours per week in the classroom and in their offices. They also have other commitments, such as departmental and institutional governance and advising.

Librarians are required to spend 40 hours per week on campus. Virtually all of this time is allocated to normal duties. Some institutions apportion a nominal amount of time to research and writing, but librarians invariably find that a meeting, an impatient patron, or a rush cataloging job takes precedence over their current research projects. Since promotion and tenure decisions are based in part on research and publication, this is an unfair situation.

If librarians are to be fully accepted as equal members of their academic faculties, they must do precisely what is expected of other professors: "teach" (i.e., perform their normal duties), serve (on committees and through advising), and publish substantive material in legitimate journals and through recognized publishing houses. The ambitious and motivated will always find the opportunity for writing during their own time, but some adjustment should be made for the majority of academic librarians who have other personal commitments. Thirty hours per week for library duties and 10 for research would be a norm for which academic librarians could strive. Once the research and writing are completed, the potential publications of faculty should never be scrutinized by the administration. This is blatant censorship, and flies in the face of both ALA-sanctioned principles and academic freedom. Finally, it is imperative that librarians maintain their competence by attending conferences, by participating in seminars, and especially by continuing their education through regular courses. Allowances for these activities must be made by all administrators, regardless of size or type of library.

CHILDREN

Children are a joy, but they sometimes can make life difficult for the professional librarian. Parents, especially of young children, are always there hovering in the background, waiting to pounce on sexually explicit books, violent videos, or pamphlets on the pleasures of recreational drugs. Sometimes they come to the library and guide their youngsters through school projects. Occasionally, parents come to the library to do their children's work for them. This even occurs in large university collections. All six respondents to the query, "How do public libraries deal with parents doing research for their children?" insisted that this is not a problem: Librarians should aid in whatever way they can. Two respondents did feel that it is unethical for parents to do this but that there is nothing a library can do about it. ("Parents," 668)

Primary and secondary school teachers sometimes give large numbers of students the same assignments. This wreaks havoc with the limited resources of any collection. Agnes Ann Hede complains about trivial questions that students cannot possibly answer unaided. This burden is compounded by a dilemma: Once the librarian knows the source or answer, what approach should he or she take with the dozens of other students who come flocking to the desk in search of the same source or answer? (42, 43)

BOOK REVIEWS

Book reviews are used as a basis for selection in smaller collections. In large libraries, they are at least partially abjured in favor of approval plans. But even in the largest facility, it is important to peruse reviews of multivolume, encyclopedic reference tools, since these can be duplicative and expensive. A judicious decision can be made based on two brief reviews or one in-depth commentary.

Writing enticing and useful reviews is an art that comes with experience and practice. An excellent though relatively brief comparative essay can take weeks to create. It is often necessary to skim or carefully read two or three other volumes before one attacks the book under consideration. To write a review without fully reading a regular book or without scrupulously scanning and evaluating a reference tool is, despite the frequency of the practice, unconscionable and a disservice to readers, colleagues, and the profession generally.

It is probably unwise to attempt to review volumes written either by friends or enemies, since objectivity would be difficult to maintain. A. J. Walford provides some excellent guidelines, in a brief 1982 essay, for those interested in pursuing this subject.

CASE STUDY

Library services were changing, and Jason Pinton, head of public services at a large municipal library in California, wanted to make a contribution. He was an innovator. Even while still in school he had been dissatisfied with the traditional service orientation of public libraries. He had always felt that many people who could benefit from a library were never reached—all those who were barely literate, unable to read English, disabled, too busy, too old, and too far away. In 1978, Pinton set up a small outreach program, but he knew that it was only an insignificant beginning.

During his 1981 summer vacation, he read Emmett and Catherine Davis's book, *Mainstreaming Library Service for Disabled People*, and it changed the course of his professional life. These authors insist that it is ethically incumbent on librarians to reach out to the disabled and the many other groups that do not benefit from proferred services.

Pinton decided to expand his program to include the disabled as well as the many people who never thought of using the library. He began to purchase some inexpensive items—Braille books and magazines, special desks for wheelchair patrons, and so on. Next he contacted appropriate local groups and organizations to publicize the new services and to solicit help and encouragement. The response was enthusiastic. In all of this he had the strongest support from his own staff as well as from the library director.

But for Pinton, who had become obsessed with the outreach program, what he had accomplished was still inadequate. He wanted to purchase a mobile library vehicle that would accommodate disabled patrons and a Kurzweil reading machine so that blind people could listen to books; he wanted to hire a specially trained librarian who would venture out into communities in order to serve those who did not visit the premises.

These big plans required lots of money, which was not available. So, with the dubious approval of the director, he began a fund-raising campaign. Somehow he managed to do all of this new work while continuing to perform his regular duties. He spoke to groups, companies, and volunteers, and after some months, a bit of money began to trickle in, but it was inadequate for Pinton's grand schemes. He persevered and even spoke to the library's board of trustees. Nevertheless, after a full year, there still was not enough money to fund even one of the major projects. He pushed harder, and began to annoy some people.

One day the director called him in. He indicated that what Pinton was attempting to do was certainly commendable, but that full service to all was an impossibility. Money was limited, no new funding was forthcoming, the regular patrons had to be served, and the kind of outreach program that Pinton envisioned was an ideal that never could be reached. Furthermore, the director had begun to receive complaints from local people who were being alienated by this big fuss over a few unserved citizens.

At this point Pinton lost his temper. "Every member of the community is entitled to our services—legally, politically, and ethically. It does not matter if someone is incapable of reading or traveling or even desiring. Additionally, many are not even citizens. Many migrant workers and their children, whom we could help immeasurably, happen to be aliens. They also are far from the central city and move around. What we need is a stronger commitment from the board and the administration. We need more money."

The director was hurt by this, since he was basically in agreement with Pinton's goals, but he pointed out that there were other patrons to serve and other problems to solve. The upshot of the meeting was that Pinton should let the outreach program simmer for a while, and return to his other duties, which recently had begun to suffer slightly.

Pinton had regained his composure, but he politely refused to give up. He insisted that he would persevere with his mission. The director said that would be acceptable, but if things got out of hand, Pinton would have to desist, or the director would have no choice but to recommend his termination.

1. Why do public facilities fail to provide for these nontraditional patrons?
2. Why can't this administration make some dramatic changes?
3. Is Pinton overreacting? Should he persevere, if it means the loss of his job?
4. What else could large, well-funded libraries do to help the unserved?

CASE STUDY

At the end of her third year as a collection development librarian at a major New York City university, Marnie Yuler received an evaluation of her work. Her immediate supervisor complimented her on her contributions to the development of the collection and university and community service. She then went on to remind Yuler that research and publication were mandatory in order to be considered for tenure. She only had two years left in which to publish some substantive articles. Yuler was aware that she was required to publish, but she had been so busy that she had put it out of her mind. Now she realized that she needed to start writing immediately and have some good luck in placing the pieces and getting them quickly into print. Otherwise, her other contributions would be for nothing, because at this university tenure was never awarded without publication.

It was hard enough for teaching faculty, who had many spare hours they could allocate to writing. Librarians had a 40-hour-per-week commitment, and most of that time was given over to their normal duties. Only three hours per week was set aside for research, and a meeting or a problem always seemed to intervene just when Yuler finally planned to get down to work. In any case, three hours per week was completely inadequate for the substantive publications demanded at her prestigious institution.

Many of her colleagues had received tenure years ago, when the requirements were much less stringent. The more recent candidates had had a difficult time of it. Yuler realized that she would either have to devote a substantial amount of work time to research and writing, thereby detracting from her collection-development duties, or try to squeeze some work into her precious free time in the evenings or on weekends, all of which she spent with her husband and two young daughters.

During the next four months, she worked on a large research project, preparing her survey instrument, making preliminary inquiries, doing the mailing, and tabulating the results. At the same time, she began to write a second essay based on research she had done years before, when she was a doctoral student. As she progressed in her writing, she regressed in her other duties. Furthermore, her formerly placid family life was in constant turmoil, because she spent only a minimal amount of time with her husband and children. Evenings and most weekends were spent at her office.

About six months after she began these two projects, disaster struck. First, her supervisor informed her that her collection-development duties were being neglected. And second, her husband hinted rather strongly that he was at the end of his tether.

Yuler was in a quandary. She could stop writing and thereby improve her other work as well as her home life, or she could continue to write and cause harm on the other two fronts. Publication, she realized, was of little value if she lost her job or her family. And this was only the beginning. Tenure, promotion, merit pay, and prestige all depended on continual research. This was not what she had had in mind when she chose librarianship as her vocation.

1. Does a situation like this have to occur?
2. How could it be avoided?
3. How could Yuler's dilemma be resolved?
4. What would you do if you were Yuler?

Chapter 9
Consulting, Freelancing, and
Information Brokerage

CONSULTING

Some time ago, perceptive information specialists and educators realized that library administrators were unable to do certain things on their own. Administrators who had never supervised the construction of a new building or the installation of an automated system could not proceed unaided. Those people with knowledge, skills, and entrepreneurial ambition went into the consulting business, on their own or in conjunction with some established firm. Many of these consultants remain information specialists, but supplement their regular salaries by providing guidance to those who need it.

Consultants, especially those with divided professional loyalties, must be on constant guard against potential abuse or unethical activities. Since consultants are regulated neither by educational nor legal requirements, anyone can claim competency. College acquisitions librarians who have supervised the successful installation of a small online catalog or circulation system are not necessarily automation experts. They might think that their knowledge is more than adequate to begin advising others. But they may quickly discover that they are not prepared for even a slightly different situation, which accordingly requires different hardware, software, and so on. If their first job is five or 10 times as complex as their only previous experience, they will be incapable of producing excellent results. At the same time, human nature probably will prevent them from admitting their inadequacies and turning the job over to more competent consultants. The point here is to be keenly aware of one's capabilities and limitations. To succeed, a consultant must be competent, knowledgeable, fair, and objective.

The most difficult hurdle that part-time consultants face is avoiding conflicts of interest. They are working for the library and not for their regular employer, a vendor, or a particular system. They should be aware of comparable systems and able to choose the one that most fully meets the required specifications. Remunerative arrangements between consultants and vendors never should be permitted, nor should consultants have a financial interest in the company producing a recommended system. The regular employer should not attempt to influence a part-time consultant's recommendations.

The consultant probably should treat the two pursuits as entirely separate entities. This means never bringing consulting homework to his or her regular place of employment or even discussing external problems with colleagues or supervisors. Conversely, the regular job should neither intrude upon nor influence the consultant's outside activities. In such a precarious situation, one can easily and inadvertently be seduced into unethical actions. Once this occurs, it is equally simple to rationalize a kickback, an influenced recommendation, or the resubmission of a final report that has already been submitted on a previous consultantship.

Because of such problems, Jose-Marie Griffiths points out, librarians now frequently require performance bonds, which are quite difficult for most consultants to post. She concludes that these bonds may merely "deter potential consultants from bidding." (115)

In 1983 the Library Association and the Institute of Information Scientists ratified a consultants' code. It is a well-meaning document, but the British have not found it overly useful for the usual reasons: It contains no penalties, and it is unenforceable. Some of those involved in the creation of this code now think that consultants should be registered. In cases in which they fail to live up to the guidelines, they would be deregistered (Gurnsey, 59, 60), which would result in an inability to practice their profession.

Those who have considered an analogous code for American practitioners are not especially optimistic. Susan Baerg Epstein, raises many pertinent problems in a brief but incisive discussion. She begins by questioning the feasibility of developing, using, and enforcing a code, since codes usually deal with absolutes while avoiding the very issues that present the most trouble. They are therefore impractical, as well as unenforceable. (115, 116) She cites a number of examples, including the necessity for attending vendors' informational breakfasts; using information gained in one context for another job (which gives an unfair advantage to the client over the vendor); offering product information not contained in the proposal; worrying about who will provide consultant services to a vendor when she refuses the job on ethical grounds; and adapting earlier work for another client. (116)

There are no clear-cut solutions to these and similar problems, which is why it is so difficult to create a useable set of ethical guidelines for consultants.

FREELANCING

Consultants generally limit their services to oral advice, a written report, or a request for proposal (the document submitted to a vendor). Freelancing librarians may do basic research, extensive document preparation, writing, editing, or information provision, especially through online database searching.

The major ethical problem for freelancers to avoid is conflict of interest. The tasks that they agree to do should not impinge upon their regular duties. It is as unacceptable to spend long evening and weekend hours on a project and therefore be physically and mentally unfit for work at one's regular place of employment as it is to do the freelance work on the employer's time. Freelancers should not lure patrons away from free or inexpensive services with the promise that they can provide superior information for a fee. And they should not use the employer's equipment to do database searching, even if they have their own passwords (and thus will be charged personally), unless a supervisor with legitimate authority has ok'd the arrangement.

Most freelancers who are serious about their work will eventually acquire their own equipment and pursue these private ventures away from their libraries. This is the preferable situation. Years ago, before the competition between academic and public libraries and commercial information brokers was so intense, even a student who owned a personal computer and a modem could go into the information business, and sometimes profitably. Now, despite the increase in need, it is much more difficult to do this.

INFORMATION BROKERAGE

Information has always made a difference. Those who knew something that their peers, enemies, or competitors did not had the edge, won the battle, or sold more products. Storehouses of information existed in the ancient Near and Far East, and tablets, rolls, stones, and leaves were consulted whenever necessary. Nevertheless, it is only recently that information has become so powerful. Not having a key fact or concept can mean the difference between success and failure. Librarians are no longer able to keep up with the demand for all forms of information, especially from the business sector.

Steven Flax, in a 1984 article, shows to what peculiar extremes companies will go to discover things about their competition. Thus, the traditional sources of information—books, journals, databases, and personal contacts—are taken for granted as basic necessities, and companies (as well as individuals) are willing to pay well for information-gathering services.

In the early 1980s, there were about 100 information brokers in the United States. (Maranjian, 125) (The preferred term now is "fee-based information service.") By 1986 the number of companies providing information for a fee had grown to 1,400. (Field, 82) These are commercial enterprises whose primary objective is to earn a profit (rather than merely to provide a service, as libraries do), and so one might suspect that ethical considerations are slighted. This, however, turns out to be generally untrue. Some brokers have created guidelines or codes that help their employees. For example, FIND/SVP, the world's largest fee-based information service, has had a "Code of Professional Responsibility" since at least 1980. This document covers misrepresentation, confidentiality, professional behavior, and the client-broker relationship. (Mintz, 38–39, 43)

Brokers may refuse to perform illegal activities, such as industrial espionage, but the real problems are much more subtle. For example, the management at FIND/SVP—which advertises that it does research, market studies, surveys, and fills "any information need"— might accept a client interested in information gleaned from animal testing or related in some way to South Africa. However, individual researchers with strong convictions against vivisection or apartheid may balk at the assignment. There is generally another researcher who does not believe that these are heinous activities and will agree to work with the client. Thus, confrontations caused by specific subject matter apparently do not occur at FIND/SVP (Interview I). In fact, a managerial-level employee insisted that ethical problems of this nature do not occur in the New York office (Interview II). This would imply that these matters are handled discreetly.

Packaged Facts, a small New York broker (which is now owned by FIND/SVP), specializes in consumer-marketing surveys. Here, an employee claimed that ethical problems never occur. Then, almost as an afterthought, he mentioned that they had once refused to aid a law firm that wanted the company to "dig up dirt" on a labor leader (Interview III). At Strategic Intelligence Systems, a long discussion failed to turn up any ethical or legal problems (Interview IV).

On the other hand, a freelance direct-mail copywriter, who packages information (rather than provides it), indicated that he has turned down a number of potentially lucrative assignments because of their content. These include solicitations with a specific political slant, pornographic or seamy material, and a newsletter that provides serious stock market advice based on astrological computations (Interview V).

Brokers, of course, are most concerned with the protection of their sources' and their clients' confidentiality. Businesses are especially fond of learning about their competition without indicating they are doing so. A broker who cannot be trusted will lose valuable personal contacts, and clients will go elsewhere. The loss of even one major account, which often keeps a broker on retainer, could be a serious financial blow.

If practitioners are not overly concerned with ethical problems, theoreticians certainly are. The perusal of just two arbitrarily chosen issues of the *Journal of Fee-Based Information Services* turned up two pertinent essays. Kay Todd notes the strange example of a broker refusing to allow the use of a letterhead (passim), and Peter Marx, an attorney, warns that settlements for the provision of faulty information are increasing. Since brokers are individually liable, and insurance is scarce and expensive (4), this is a terrifying development. Anne P. Mintz cites the United States Supreme Court's precedent-setting Greenmoss decision, which deserves complete recapitulation:

> In Burlington, Vermont in 1976, Dun & Bradstreet employed a 16-year-old high school student as a reporter at the U.S. Federal Bankruptcy Court. When a carpenter formerly employed by Greenmoss Builders filed for personal bankruptcy the student told her employers that Greenmoss Builders had filed for bankruptcy. This information was listed in the *Business Information Report* database that subscribers tap for credit reports and caused Greenmoss Builders actual damages. Their creditors and insurance companies had cause for concern, in addition to business which was lost due to the erroneous information.
>
> In the lawsuit brought by Greenmoss Builders against Dun & Bradstreet, a jury awarded $350,000, including $300,000 punitive damages. Dun & Bradstreet appealed not the verdict, since they never denied that the report was in error, but the award of punitive damages. They argued that under the First Amendment, the plaintiff must prove "actual malice"—that the false statement was made without regard for the truth. While the case was tried on grounds of libel and first amendment guarantees of freedom of speech to commercial and economic ventures, the underlying situation is a glaring example of information malpractice on the part of Dun & Bradstreet. This case was appealed by Dun & Bradstreet all the way to the U.S. Supreme Court, where the case was heard in early October 1984, and decided in late June 1984. [*sic*] (43)

The decision in this case upholds my contention that providers of information must bear responsibility for their actions. Furthermore, it shows that malpractice suits against information purveyors are no longer merely hypothetical.

Commercial vendors of information have discovered and cultivated a lucrative market by aiming at specific needs, reformulating the same information in different ways, and being aggressive. (Field, 82–83) They provide expensive information upon which the customer bases important decisions. They therefore must bear responsibility for the completeness and accuracy of what is tendered. If errors derive from an unverifiable source, e.g., pages of inaccurate or obsolete statistics produced by a numeric database producer or vendor, then it seems to me that the broker cannot be held liable. In that case, culpability devolves on the database producer or the vendor. Warnings concerning accuracy can be affixed to the tendered data, to protect both the broker and the client from suits because of misinformation.

Information brokers correctly believe that they have the same rights as individuals when it comes to using the resources of public, academic, and even some special libraries. And although they easily can abuse these rights by making many complex demands upon the limited resources of, for example, a small public collection, librarians agree that brokers should not be discriminated against.

This is the consensus of the five respondents to the query (in *American Libraries*): Should libraries render the same free services to regular patrons and commercial information brokers? Four were unequivocal in their affirmation that the librarian exists to provide information. One person did indicate that this should be a reciprocal arrangement, although he did not provide any details. ("Should," 288)

In a personal interview, a librarian at Rensselaer Polytechnic Institute (RPI) recounted an excellent example of how commercial information specialists can take advantage of a library's generosity. RPI maintains copies of some famous reports, which they recopy for patrons. Information brokers from all over the United States request these, pay only the copying costs, and then sell them to their clients. This procedure raises another problem: If library personnel spend too much time serving external clients, they will not have adequate time to help their regular patrons; in this case, RPI students and faculty (Interview VI).

Patrick M. O'Brien presents a slightly different perspective on the broker-library relationship. About 20 years ago, when information brokers began to make extensive use of free public, academic, and special library services, the Minneapolis Public Library created Inform, which provided businesses with information at a cost of $25 per hour. Two purposes were served here. First, patrons who were willing to pay were given extra, in-depth service. Second, brokers who might have abused their rights by monopolizing library services were no longer able to do so. This early instance of library information provision for a fee was widely discussed, but, strangely enough, it was only infrequently "criticized as inappropriate." (123, 124) All of this implies that it is ethically acceptable for commercial-information people to make use of free public facilities and services, as long as they do not abuse their rights or monopolize the librarians.

CASE STUDY

George Soman began his professional career as a reference librarian/collection developer at an excellent Midwestern college, where the challenges were counterbalanced by a great deal of freedom. After five years, his wife received a medical residency at a New York hospital, so they moved to the city. Library positions were scarce, but Soman quickly found a job with a small, private company that specialized in providing information to individuals and firms for a substantial fee. Because there was an ever-growing need for these private information services, the competition for business was increasing.

Soman enjoyed the new work, which differed greatly from his previous duties. He was especially gratified to be earning much more money, which helped make it possible to live in New York City with its high cost of living. He, naturally, was disappointed to lose his long vacation and the academic freedom associated with college employment.

Soman gathered information from various sources, including databases, telephone conversations, and personal observations and interviews. After only seven months, through diligence and perseverance, he began to make a strong impression on the firm.

One morning, he had a call from a new client, a small pharmaceutical company interested in producing a powerful new antidepressant that would be used in controlling schizophrenia. The side effects, however, were extremely negative. Because the drug was so new, there was not much information available through the normal channels (*Chemical Abstracts*, Medline, etc.). The pharmaceutical firm wanted Soman to do some personal searching at other companies and academic institutions. The negative effects of the drug were of especial interest.

Soman did some preliminary work and discovered that much of what was known had been found through horrible tests performed on laboratory animals, including dogs and chimpanzees. There even had been some experiments performed on incarcerated human subjects without their informed consent.

Soman contacted his employer and told him that he would be unable to continue with the project. The purposeful harming of the animals was grounds enough for refusing to help the pharmaceutical company learn more about this drug. That was compounded by the failure to acquire informed consent from the human subjects.

Because it was such a small firm, there was no one else available to do this job. Had there been, the owner, Lester Oring, explained, there would have been no real problem. In fact, Oring sympathized with Soman's position and, additionally, was quite impressed with his defense of an ethical position. At the same time, he adhered to the dictum that information-service personnel must provide information regardless of content. If an individual employee cannot work in a particular area, he explained, that was okay, as long as someone else could. Since this was not possible in this case, Soman must continue with the research. Soman politely refused to do so.

The discussion continued for more than two hours. Oring finally concluded that he would think about his options and render a decision the following morning. He might be forced to fire Soman and hire someone able to provide information without considering requests in an ethical context. In business, lamentably, ethics and even legality sometimes had to be subservient to service, products, and, ultimately, profit.

1. Do you suppose this type of situation arises frequently?
2. Do you think Soman is acting correctly in principle—in this instance?
3. Should Soman relent, if Oring informs him that he plans to fire him?
4. Is Oring a hypocrite?

CASE STUDY

In December 1975, Loun's Chemical Products, a large company whose offices and plant are located far from any major city, hired Deborah Linckson as their first full-time professional librarian. Her duties included selection of reference tools, books, and journals; database searching; SDI; ILL; and research and report writing, when necessary.

This took up almost all of Linckson's time. The collection had been neglected for a while, and many of the reference books were dated and newer editions had to be ordered. Additionally, the firm was in the process of expanding its product lines, and many chemists as well as marketing and sales personnel required online searches and notification of new, pertinent articles as they arrived in the latest issues of journals.

Linckson fulfilled requests quickly and pleasantly. She even began to circulate a photocopied compilation of the tables of contents of 25 of the most important journals. She produced "Linckson's Current Contents" in multiple copies once a month and endeared herself to virtually every professional employee. She never turned a patron away or excused herself because she was too busy. She made the time to help everyone. Despite this, she did not let her professional duties impinge upon her personal life.

One day, Jack Blane, a pleasant senior chemist, approached Linckson. He explained that he was working on a bibliographic survey of material related to the life and times of Louis Pasteur, a project that had nothing to do with his job, but which had fascinated him for some time. He was now about to get down to serious work, and he wondered whether Linckson would be able to do some searching and research for him on her own time, for which he would be glad to pay her. Her immediate and positive response was heartening, because Blane had downplayed his interest in this project. He had been obsessed with Pasteur for years, and this bibliography was his primary passion. Linckson began to produce a plethora of excellent items, at night and on weekends, and Blane was kept busy and happy.

Some months after she had begun to work for Blane, another employee requested Linckson's private services. Once again she immediately acquiesced. Soon she was doing a substantial amount of freelance work, not only for Loun's Chemical people, but also for local clients who lived in the surrounding communities. Because she charged a considerable fee for each job, she had almost doubled her modest income.

One cold morning Flannary Rusk, Linckson's supervisor, asked to speak with her. Rusk wondered why there had been such a dramatic increase in online costs during the past few months. Linckson explained that she had been doing some personal work on her own time and that she had kept a precise record. Now that the bills had begun to arrive, she would pay her share.

Rusk objected vehemently to this and said that she would speak with the vice president for internal management about it. "Why didn't you ask about this before you began?" she asked.

"It never occurred to me that the management would object to my use of the equipment. Indeed, I still do not understand the problem," Linckson replied.

Two days later, two vice presidents, Rusk, and Linckson had a long talk. Linckson learned that the company strongly frowned on what she was doing. They objected to her freelance work generally, and specifically to the use of company equipment and passwords. In fact, it appeared to them that this was a classic case of conflict of interest. Linckson defended herself, proclaiming her innocence and insisting that no conflict had occurred. The senior vice president disagreed and asked her to stop doing freelance work, which made Linckson a very unhappy woman.

1. Did Linckson act unethically by not consulting her supervisor before she began to use company equipment for personal profit?
2. Did the management overreact?
3. There are many viable solutions to Linckson's problem. Discuss at least three.

Chapter 10
Conclusion

Ethics has never played more than a minimal role in librarianship. Recently, however, because the public has become aware of unsavory activity in virtually every arena, ethical considerations have assumed a more prominent role in the world of information services. The obligations of information providers therefore have increased in both number and complexity.

Perhaps the most difficult and controversial dilemma faced by librarians is the duality of social responsibility on the one hand and the necessity to defend intellectual freedom on the other; that is, the antagonism between advocacy and neutrality. It would be useful if this volume could mediate between these two positions, but there are times when they are so antithetical that only the individual can make a choice.

From the purely professional perspective, that choice has already been made for the practitioner. The ALA, through the code, the *Library Bill of Rights*, and the *Freedom to Read Statement*, calls for a defense of intellectual freedom. But those interested in social melioration cannot always conform to that ideal. At any rate, compliance with all principles, dicta, and regulations is voluntary, since there are no enforcement measures in effect. The consequences of noncompliance are minimal, although malpractice accusations are becoming more common. Actual suits against libraries or personnel are rare or nonexistent, but there have been a few decisions rendered against commercial information brokers.

Librarians claim to be professionals. They are generally accorded the appropriate privileges and status that accompany this designation, although they are sometimes remunerated at a less than professional level. Some university, special, and even a limited number of public librarians are fairly compensated, but many school and public personnel do not receive a decent salary. This is especially true for librarians in the earliest stages of their careers.

Individuals, groups, and the ALA should lobby for minimum salary standards. Professionals deserve fair compensation for their five or six years of higher education, accumulated knowledge, and skill. The image of someone accepting a professional position for $15,000 per year is extremely negative, especially at a time when new law school graduates can command four times that sum.

As professionals, librarians have certain extraordinary obligations to their clients, but these may never contravene ordinary ethical dicta. The principles, rules, and regulations under which librarians function should not protect and enhance the librarian at the expense of the client (as is often the case in other professions).

Despite the adamant position maintained by most commentators and professional organizations concerning the necessity for providing requested information in a objective way (by refusing to allow personal beliefs or harmful possibilities to intervene between librarian and patron), practitioners are sometimes upset by specific experiences. They may even refuse to help the client. B. Strickland-Hodge elaborates on this:

> I hope to show that there are times when the librarian or information officer is faced with an ethical question which, if he is to maintain a professional role, necessitates the refusal of direct information assistance and requires the client to be referred to a third party whether or not the required information is available to the librarian. (129)

There follows the example of a doctor and pharmacist refusing to divulge the purpose of a drug to a patient, who then repairs to the public library, where he or she may receive incorrect information that results in deleterious consequences. (130) The author then concludes:

> The ethical considerations of information dissemination should concern us all. The reference librarian will be faced with ethical questions and it is not sufficient to brush them aside claiming information of all types is free for all. The professional bodies which govern information dissemination should consider that ethical judgements perhaps leading to the withholding of certain types of information to certain individuals show a professional attitude to information work. (131)

This is an unusual stance, one that is defended infrequently in the literature. Strickland-Hodge is a British educator, not a practitioner, and that might help to explain this firm, iconoclastic advocacy of information control. Melissa Watson, faced with a different situation, did refuse to help:

> A case in point occurred to me several years ago, in fact, its similarity to Hauptman's [1976 bomb] experiment was striking. Two boys entered the public library in which I was working and asked if we had any books which had information on building bottle bombs. They indicated that they thought it would be great fun to construct a few and explode them in the city dump. The other librarian on

duty and I exchanged looks, and then said that we had only one book on the subject and that it had been checked out for some time. The young men, who were not too bright, cheerfully accepted this bit of information and went on their way. According to some of the standards already mentioned, the behavior of the other librarian and myself had been highly unethical. In all likelihood we could have found that information for those boys; we had simply determined that we were not going to provide it to them. Why? Because we knew them by reputation to be troublemakers (one was sent to a reform school some time later), and because we had figured that it was only a few steps from exploding things at the dump to blowing up city hall—or the book drop, for that matter. We had based our service on a value judgement of the user and had withheld the information, which would seem to be a violation of the RASD's ethics code. Yet at the time we felt justified in our actions because we felt a greater responsibility to the safety of our community rather than to our profession. (119)

But unlike Strickland-Hodge, Watson is not willing to extrapolate any generalizations concerning the withholding of information. In fact, she is not certain that what she did was correct, and the situation (and its ethical implications) disturbed her. (119)

It has been pointed out that the protection of confidentiality in all areas of information service is of the utmost importance. Circulated materials, reference queries, and database searches are all private matters, the details of which must not be revealed except with the patron's permission or under the duress of a subpoena. Even in this latter case, questions should be posed to make certain that the court really wants a breach of confidentiality to take place.

Angela C. Million and Kim N. Fisher suggest that libraries now need a written confidentiality policy. (346) Attempts by various individuals, organizations, and government agencies to solicit confidential information from libraries have become so commonplace that, as Million and Fisher indicate, 32 states have laws that protect library records from snoopers. (347) Backed by the ALA, the profession's stance, a written policy, and in many cases legal directive, patron confidentiality easily can be protected. It is ironic that librarians, who are obligated to provide free access to information, concurrently must protect transactional information of a private nature. Extremely personal information, which most people would want protected—lists compiled by companies that monitor people's political and religious affiliations, and financial, medical, and insurance records (Linowes 491–492)—is not available in libraries, nor should it be. Law librarians must be especially diligent in protecting the confidences of patrons. Litigants doing their own legal work may inadvertently reveal potentially damaging or even life-threatening details to a librarian. This information must not be mentioned to anyone, including colleagues, patrons, friends, and relatives.

Conflict of interest in general library work, consulting, and free-lancing is always a potential danger. Norman D. Stevens believes that "we have accepted and adopted marginal practices that we somehow regard as normal, but should not." (50) Many of his examples involve conflict of interest, with an emphasis on personal financial gain. For example, the producers of salable items may present or publish papers on the items' usefulness to libraries; vendors can entice individuals with financial allurements; or information specialists sometimes also work as paid board members of firms that offer products to libraries, including the information specialist's library. (50)

Conflicts also can occur on a more mundane level. Institutional facilities, services, equipment, and supplies should be used with the utmost discretion when writing for profit, communicating with professional friends, or working for a professional journal or organization, as an editor or official, for example. Costs for these external endeavors can be astronomical, one's employer may not be in the position to subsidize them, despite their usefulness, importance, and prestige.

Information dispensing, confidentiality, and conflict of interest are the three primary areas of ethical concern in librarianship. There are also peripherial problems, many of which have been discussed in this book. N. J. Belkin and S. E. Robertson strangely suggest that there are areas in which theoretical research in information science should be delimited. They fear the misapplication of research results in propaganda, advertising, and gender-oriented education. (cited in Kostrewski, 279)

Even more peculiar is the blatant dishonesty practiced at the highest levels. It is virtually incomprehensible that people would work diligently for many years to advance professionally and then destroy everything that they had accomplished by sexually harassing someone or misappropriating books or funds. Nevertheless, these activities occur with astonishing frequency. The normal concerns of professional ethics in librarianship pale in comparison with the enormity of such activities. Basic honesty, diligence, and consideration ought to be givens. The ethical problems that are inevitable occur because one often has to make a choice between two equally difficult possibilities, such as professional obligations and societal needs, both of which deserve strict attention:

> For too long, information scientists in their work have tended to disassociate themselves from the outside world. They need to realise that the consequences of actions taken by their organisations can, and often do, have far-reaching effects on society at large and it is their duty to be aware of such consequences. (Kostrewski, 282)

This is a position with which Irving Klempner undoubtedly would agree. His incisive comment provides a fitting conclusion to this book:

It would seem irresponsible for an information professional not to consider and weigh carefully the overall human and social implications of decisions affecting system design and its services. The quantification, detachment, and objectivity called for in modern science cannot mitigate or relieve us of our responsibility. It is a responsibility in which we must not fail. (162)

Bibliography

Anderson, Charles. "The Myth of the Expert Searcher." *Library Journal*, February 1, 1986: 37–39.

Asheim, Lester. "Not Censorship but Selection." *Wilson Library Bulletin*, September 1953: 63–67.

Bayles, Michael D. *Professional Ethics*. Belmont, CA: Wadsworth, 1981.

Bekker, Johan. "Professional Ethics and Its Application to Librarianship." Diss. Case Western Reserve University, 1976.

Berman, Sanford. "DDC 19: An Indictment." In his *The Joy of Cataloging: Essays, Letters, Reviews, and Other Explosions*. Phoenix, AZ: Oryx Press, 1981, pp. 177–185.

Blazek, Ron. "User Fees: A Survey of Public and Academic Reference Librarians." *The Reference Librarian*, 4 (1982): 55–74.

Bledstein, Burton J. *The Culture of Professionalism*. New York: Norton, 1976.

Borsch, Frederick H. "It Is Often Difficult Helping Students Learn More About Values and Ethics." *The Chronicle of Higher Education*, September 5, 1984: 104.

Brichford, Maynard J. "Seven Sinful Thoughts." *The American Archivist*, 43 (1) (Winter 1980): 13–16.

"Censorship in the Name of Public Health." *American Libraries*, May 1986: 306.

Clarke, Jack. "Reference Ethics—Do We Need Them?" *The Reference Librarian*, 4 (1982): 25–30.

Cleghorn, Reese. "When Readers Become Suspect." *Library Lit. The Best of 1970*, eds. Bill Katz, Joel J. Schwartz. Metuchen, NJ: Scarecrow, 1971, pp. 398–404.

"A Code of Ethics for Archivists." *The American Archivist*, 43 (3) (Summer 1980): 414–415.

"A Commitment to Information Services: Developmental Guidelines." *RQ*, 18 (3) (Spring 1979): 275–278.

Crawford, Helen. "In Search of an Ethic of Medical Librarianship." *Bulletin of the Medical Library Association*, 66 (3) (July 1978): 331–337.

Cromley, Allan. "Term Given for Stealing Rare Books/Former OU Official Sentenced." *The Saturday Oklahoman*, December 1, 1984.

Crowley, Terence. "Half-Right Reference: Is It True?" *RQ*, 25 (1) (Fall 1985): 59–68.

Davis, Emmett. "The Ethics of Information Serving Homo Sapiens vs. Homo Biblios." *The Reference Librarian*, 4 (1982): 31–43.

Dowd, Robert C. "Will Your Library Teach Me How to Freebase Cocaine? Or Yet Another Unobtrusive Test of Reference Performance." *The Reference Librarian*, forthcoming.

Durrance, Joan C. "The Generic Librarian: Anonymity vs. Accountability." *RQ*, 22 (3) (Spring 1983): 278–283.

———. "Toward the Development of an Informed Citizenry." *The Reference Librarian*, 4 (1982): 45–54.

Epstein, Susan Baerg. "Problems with Ethical Standards." In "Ethics in the Library Automation Process: A Forum." *Library Hi Tech*, 4 (4) (Winter 1986): 115–117.

Farley, Judith. "Reference Ethics: A True Confession." *The Reference Librarian*, 4 (1982): 13–17.

"FBI Subpoenas SUNY for Search Records." *Library Journal*, April 15, 1987: 15.

"Feminism and Censorship: Strange Bedfellows?" New York: F.A.C.T.: Feminist Anti Censorship Taskforce, n.d. (Leaflet.)

Field, Anne R. and Catherine L. Harris. "The Information Business." *Business Week*, August 25, 1986: 82–86, 90.

Fish, Stanley. "Anti-Professionalism." *New Literary History*, 17 (1) (Autumn 1985): 89–107.

Flanagan, Leo N. "Defending the Indefensible: The Limits of Intellectual Freedom." *Library Journal*, October 15, 1975: 1887–1891.

Flax, Steven. "How to Snoop on Your Competitors." *Fortune*, May 14, 1984: 28–33.

Foskett, D. J. *The Creed of a Librarian: No Politics, No Religion, No Morals.* London: Library Association, 1962.

Geer, Judith. "Librarian Closes Book on Feds." *American Libraries*, October 1985: 18.

Griffiths, Jose-Marie. "Formal Standards." In "Ethics in the Library Automation Process: A Forum." *Library Hi Tech*, 4 (4) (Winter 1986): 113–115.

Gurnsey, John. "The U.K. Code of Practice for Consultants: A Partial Solution." *Library Hi Tech*, 4 (4) (Winter 1986): 59–62.

Hauptman, Robert. "Ethical Commitment and the Professions." *Catholic Library World*, December 1979: 196–199.

———. "Professionalism or Culpability? An Experiment in Ethics." *Wilson Library Bulletin*, 50 (8) (April 1976): 626–627.

Hede, Agnes Ann. "The Ethics of Trivia." *Library Journal*, April 1, 1986: 42–43.

Hill, Fred and Robert Hauptman. "Deride, Abide, or Dissent: On the Ethics of Professional Conduct." Unpublished paper.

House, David E. "Reference Efficiency or Reference Deficiency." *Library Association Record*, 76 (11) (November 1974): 222–223.

Intellectual Freedom Manual. Chicago: American Library Association, 1983.

Interview I. In person interview, July 8, 1987, New York City, with male FIND/SVP employee who preferred to remain anonymous.

Interview II. Telephone interview, July 9, 1987, New York City, with female FIND/SVP employee who preferred to remain anonymous.

Interview III. In person interview, July 9, 1987, New York City, with male Packaged Facts employee who preferred to remain anonymous.

Interview IV. In person interview, July 10, 1987, New York City, with male Strategic Intelligence Systems employee who preferred to remain anonymous.

Interview V. In person interview, July 11, 1987, New York City, with male freelance advertising specialist who preferred to remain anonymous.

Interview VI. In person interview, July 14, 1987, Albany, New York, with female Rensselaer Polytechnic Institute librarian who preferred to remain anonymous.

"Is It Ethical to Help a Student Find a How-to-Commit-Suicide Manual, and Is That All You Do?" *American Libraries*, November 1983: 643.

Isbell, Mary K. and M. Kathleen Cook. "Confidentiality of Online Bibliographic Searches: Attitudes and Practices." *RQ*, 25 (4) (Summer 1986): 483–487.

Kanner, Bernice. "What Price Ethics? The Morality of the Eighties." *New York*, July 14, 1986: 28–34.

Kant, Immanuel. *Fundamental Principles of the Metaphysics of Morals*. Indianapolis, IN: Bobbs-Merrill, 1949.

Kirkwood, C.C. and Tim J. Watts. "Legal Reference Service: Duties v. Liabilities." *Legal Reference Services Quarterly*, 3 (2) (Summer 1983): 67–82.

Klempner, Irving M. "Information Technology and Personal Responsibility." *Special Libraries*, 72 (2) (April 1981): 157–162.

Knight, Lydia F. Letter: "Professional or Personal Ethics?" *Library Journal*, July 1985: 9.

Kochen, Manfred. "Ethics and Information Science." *Journal of the American Society for Information Science*, 38 (3) (May 1987): 206–210.

Kostrewski, B. J. and Charles Oppenheim. "Ethics in Information Science." *Journal of Information Science*, 1 (5) (January 1980): 277–283.

Kultgen, John. "The Ideological Use of Professional Codes." *Business and Professional Ethics Journal*. 1 (3) (Spring 1982): 53–69.

"Librarian Is Charged in an Embezzlement." *New York Times*, July 18, 1987: 31.

Lindsey, Jonathan A. and Ann E. Prentice. *Professional Ethics and Librarians*. Phoenix, AZ: Oryx Press, 1985.

Linowes, David F. and Michele M. Hoyman. "Data Confidentiality, Social Research, and the Government." *Library Trends*, 30 (3) (Winter 1982): 489–503.

Manley, Will. "Facing the Public." *Wilson Library Bulletin*. February 1987: 32–33.

Maranjian, Lorig and Richard W. Boss. *Fee-Based Information Services: A Study of a Growing Industry*. New York: Bowker, 1980.

Marx, Peter. "Legal Implications of Liability for Information Providers: An Evolving Area." *Journal of Fee-Based Information Services*, 4 (3) (July/August 1986): 4.

Matthews, Joe. "Untitled." In "Ethics in the Marketplace: A Forum." *Library Hi Tech*, 4 (4) (Winter 1986): 95–97.

McFadden, Robert D. "F.B.I. in New York Asks Librarians' Aid in Reporting on Spies." *New York Times*, (September 18, 1987): A1, B2.

Milgrim, Stanley. *Obedience to Authority: An Experimental View.* New York: Harper & Row, 1962.

Million, Angela C. and Kim N. Fisher. "Library Records: A Review of Confidentiality Laws and Policies." *The Journal of Academic Librarianship,* 11 (6) (January 1986): 346–349.

Mintz, Anne P. "Information Practice and Malpractice." *Library Journal,* September 15, 1985: 38–43.

Moeller, Kathy. Telephone conversation, late January 1988, Summit, NJ, with Moeller, Overlook Hospital Librarian.

Monahan, Michael. "Untitled." In "Ethics in the Marketplace: A Forum." *Library Hi Tech,* 4 (4) (Winter 1986): 103–104.

Myers, Marcia J. and Jassim M. Jirjees. *The Accuracy of Telephone Reference/Information Services in Academic Libraries: Two Studies.* Metuchen, NJ: Scarecrow, 1983.

Newton, Lisa. "The Origin of Professionalism: Sociological Conclusions and Ethical Implications." *Business and Professional Ethics Journal,* 1 (4) (Summer 1982): 33–43.

O'Brien, Patrick M. "Some Ethical Problems of Reference Service." *The Reference Librarian,* 4 (1982): 123–127.

"Parents' Presence Poses No Problem." *American Libraries,* October 1986: 668.

Peattie, Noel. "Cardinal Mazirin Is Dead?!" *SIPAPU,* 17 (2) (Late 1986): 11–17.

———. "'Truth' and Consequences." *SIPAPU,* 16 (2) (Late 1985): 8–16.

Pringle, Daphne. Telephone conversation, late January 1988, New York City, with Pringle, New York University Medical Center Patient Librarian.

Propkop, Mary and Charles R. McClure. "The Public Librarian and Service Ethics: A Dilemma." *Public Library Quarterly,* 3 (4) (Winter 1982): 69–81.

"Rare Book Librarian Arraigned in Theft." *Library Journal,* November 1, 1986: 19.

"Reports of Physicians' Negligence Leap 44%." *USA Today,* November 19, 1986: 6A.

The Right to Information: Legal Questions and Policy Issues. Ed. Jane Varlejs. Jefferson, NC: McFarland, 1984.

Rothstein, Samuel. "In Search of Ourselves." *Library Journal,* 93 (2) (January 15, 1968): 156ff.

———. "Where Does It Hurt? Identifying the Real Concerns in the Ethics of Reference Service." *The Reference Librarian,* 4 (1982): 1–12.

Savand, Réjean. "Toward a New Model of Professionalism?" *RQ,* 25 (4) (Summer 1986): 498–505.

Schanck, Peter C. "Unauthorized Practice of Law and the Legal Reference Librarian." In "Legal Reference Service: The Delivery Process." *Law Library Journal,* 72 (1) (Winter 1979): 57–64.

Schuman, Patricia Glass. "Social Responsibility: An Agenda for the Future." *Library Journal,* January 1, 1976: 251–254.

Serebnick, Judith. "Self-Censorship by Librarians: An Analysis of Checklist-Based Research." *Drexel Library Quarterly,* 18 (1) (Winter 1982): 35–56.

Shaver, Donna B., Nancy S. Hewison, and Leslie W. Wykoff. "Ethics for Online Intermediaries." *Special Libraries*, Fall 1985: 238–245.

"Should Information Brokers Get Free Library Services?" *American Libraries*, May 1985: 288.

Shuman, Bruce A. *The River Bend Casebook: Problems in Public Library Service*. Phoenix, AZ: Oryx Press, 1981.

———. *River Bend Revisited: The Problem Patron in the Library*. Phoenix, AZ: Oryx Press, 1984.

Stahl, Wilson M. "Automation and Ethics: A View from the Trenches." *Library Hi Tech*, 4 (4) (Winter 1986): 53–57.

"Standards for Ethical Conduct for Rare Book, Manuscript, and Special Collections Librarians." (Fourth draft, March 1, 1984.) *College & Research Libraries News*, July/August 1984: 357–358.

Stevens, Norman D. "The New Ethics." *Library Hi Tech*, 4 (4) (Winter 1986), 49–51.

Stover, Mark. "Confidentiality and Privacy in Reference Service." *RQ*, Winter 1987: 240-244.

Strickland-Hodge, B. "Ethics and the Reference Librarian." *The Reference Librarian*, 4 (1982): 129–132.

Swan, John C. "Untruth or Consequences." *Library Journal*, July 1986: 44–52.

Telephone conversation. Telephone conversation, late January 1988, New York City, with female Hospital for Joint Diseases Medical Reference Librarian who preferred to remain anonymous.

Todd, Kay. "Information Brokers and Document Delivery Services: A View from the Customer's Perspective—Part II." *Journal of Fee-Based Information Services*, 4 (2) (March/April 1986): 1, 3.

Toulmin, Stephen. "The Tyranny of Principles." *The Hastings Center Report*, 11 (6) (December 1981): 31–39.

Walford, A. J. "The Reviewing of Reference Books." *The Reference Librarian*, 4 (1982): 165–169.

Watson, Melissa. "The Unresolved Conflict." *The Reference Librarian*, 4 (1982): 117–121.

West, Celeste. "The Secret Garden of Censorship: Ourselves." *Library Journal*, September 1, 1983: 1651–1653.

Wiener, Paul B. "On My Mind: Mad Bombers and Ethical Librarians: A Dialogue with Robert Hauptman and John Swan." *Catholic Library World*, 58 (4) (January/February 1987): 161–163.

Wood, M. Sandra and Beverly L. Renford. "Ethical Aspects of Medical Reference." *The Reference Librarian*, 4 (1982): 75–87.

Index

Compiled by Linda Webster

Robert Hauptman is an assistant professor at St. Cloud State University (St. Cloud, Minnesota), where he does reference work and teaches undergraduate and graduate courses in library science. He is currently coauthoring a monograph on technology and public service. He has written extensively in the areas of library science and literary criticism.